MW01251256

MANAGING CHANGE

MANAGING CHANGE *is not a theoretical publication; it offers a practical guide and case studies which very clearly demonstrate just how business can democratise the workplace and reach out to the community.*
Professor Louise Tager, Executive Director,
The Law Review Project

Business' understanding of its role in transition will be critical for the success of democratisation in South Africa. MANAGING CHANGE *helps us understand why.*
Frederick van Zyl Slabbert, Policy Director,
Institute for a Democratic Alternative for South Africa

MANAGING CHANGE *provides a clear roadmap for all businesses, large and small, through the minefield of transition.*
Spencer Sterling, President,
South African Chamber of Business (Sacob)

MANAGING CHANGE *will be of great assistance to those leaders who wish to participate in the exciting process of bringing about a just and equitable society.*
Peter Wrighton, Chairman, Premier Group

MANAGING CHANGE *provides an excellent framework for debate ... The CBM has been a valuable initiativ e in promoting discussions among business leaders about the best role that business can play during the transition.*
Clem Sunter, Chairman, Gold and Uranium Division,
Anglo American Corporation

In this exciting period of transition we urgently need a midwife to usher us into the bright new world. MANAGING CHANGE *serves that purpose.*
Jabu Mabuza, Executive President, Foundation for African Business
and Consumer Services (Fabcos)

MANAGING CHANGE

A guide to the role of business in transition

Compiled by the
Consultative Business Movement
National Team

Ravan Press  *Johannesburg*

First published by Ravan Press
PO Box 31134 Braamfontein 2017
South Africa

© Consultative Business Movement 1993

First published 1993
Second Impression 1993

ISBN 0 86975 442 4

Cover design: Hunt Lascaris TBWA
DTP setting and design: Ravan Press

Printed by Creda Press Cape Town

The authors

The CBM National Team, the authors of this publication, is comprised of (in alphabetical order):

Renee Alberts (National Organiser)

Ben Coetsee (National RoBiT Co-ordinator)

Colin Coleman (National Programmes Director)

Theuns Eloff (Executive Director)

Debra Marsden (National Economic Director)

Roddy Payne (National Socio-Economic Co-ordinator)

Contents

Acknowledgements

The authors acknowledge the important role played by the many contributors to this publication:

☐ all participants in the RoBiT workshops held in the PWV, Natal, the Western Cape and the Eastern Cape during 1991 (see full list in the appendix section).

☐ the RoBiT National Committee, which managed the RoBiT process:

Mel Palmer (Engen)	George Lindeque (Eskom)
Robbie Cox (HL&H)	Peter Campbell (Nampak)
Leon Cohen (PG Bison)	Andrew Tainton (Protea Assurance)
Terry McCulloch (Shell)	Arie van der Zwan (Southern Life)
Martin Parry (T&N Holdings)	Judy Oosthuizen (Union Spinning Mills)

☐ the CBM Regional Co-ordinators in the PWV, Natal and the Western Cape for their work in assisting the RoBiT process:
Dominic Mitchell and Gary Cullen (Natal)
Mongezi Stofile and Andrew Feinstein (PWV)
Zohra Ebrahim and Retief Olivier (Western Cape)

☐ the CBM Head Office administrative team, without which this publication would not have been possible:
Santie Mulder
Khanya Makgabo
Gillian Hutchings

The authors also thank Reg Lascaris, Jeanne Bestbier, Glenn Moss and their respective organisations for their support and advice.

List of acronyms

ANC	African National Congress
Azapo	Azanian Peoples Organisation
CBM	Consultative Business Movement
CGF	Community Growth Fund
Cosatu	Congress of South African Trade Unions
Codesa	Convention for a Democratic South Africa
CP	Conservative Party
CSI	Corporate Social Investment
DP	Democratic Party
DET	Department of Education and Training
Fabcos	Foundation for African Business and Consumer Services
GDP	Gross Domestic Product
GNP	Gross National Product
IFP	Inkatha Freedom Party
JCI	Johannesburg Consolidated Industries
JSE	Johannesburg Stock Exchange
MRCC	Mpumalanga Reconstruction Co-ordinating Committee
Nactu	National Council of Trade Unions
NEF	National Economic Forum
NGO	Non-Governmental Organisation
NHF	National Housing Forum
NP	National Party
OD	Organisational Development
PAC	Pan-Africanist Congress
Ppwawu	Paper, Pulp, Wood and Allied Workers Union
PWV	Pretoria-Witwatersrand-Vaal
REDF	Regional Economic and Development Forum
RoBiT	Role of Business in Transition
Saccola	South African Consultative Committee on Labour Affairs
SBDC	Small Business Development Corporation
SECC	Soweto Education Co-ordinating Committee
Seifsa	Steel and Engineering Industries Federation of South Africa
SME	Small and Medium Enterprise
Uwusa	United Workers Union of South Africa

Foreword

South Africa stands on the threshold of one of the most important phases in its history. Within 12 months, our country will probably have its first non-racial general election. In voting, South Africans will put a government in place that will, for the first time, be representative of all its citizens. This election will also be a watershed in the transition from centuries of colonialism and decades of apartheid to a democratic system of government.

The next period will therefore be crucial for our country's future. Not only will the multi-party negotiations have to bear constructive fruits, but the country will have to prepare for elections within a short period of time. This will include a massive amount of administration and campaigning, placing a huge responsibility on all interest groups, including political players, the government and the civil service.

The responsibility for a successful transition does not, however, rest only on the shoulders of politicians and civil servants. The rest of South African society (often referred to as 'civil society') has an essential role to play, not only in the run-up to the elections, but also in the medium term, when a new constitution is being drafted.

As an important part of civil society, the business community began to realise its responsibility in this regard some time ago. Various initiatives by business organisations, companies and individual business leaders, together with other groups, have already been undertaken. The most significant initiative which business has taken part in is no doubt the National Economic Forum, launched in October 1992. Much remains, however, to be done. If, for instance, the political transition is not accompanied by economic growth and development, South Africa will not survive the demands placed on it in the next three years. The political transition will have to be followed closely by an economic transition which broadens participation and enables all South Africans to share in the economy.

Nor will political transition alone meet the expectations of the disenfranchised, to whom freedom means not only the vote, but also jobs, land, houses and education. This is of crucial importance to business, which carries the responsibility to assist in every way it can in this transition.

It was with this in mind that the Consultative Business Movement embarked, in 1992, on a project focusing on the 'Role of Business in Transition', which in typical South African fashion created the acronym 'RoBiT'. This publication is the product of the first phase of the project, and is offered to a wider audience in the hope that it will contribute not only to the debate in business and wider circles, but also lead to business playing its rightful role in helping to make the transition successful.

Murray Hofmeyr, Neal Chapman and Mike Sander
Chairpersons: Consultative Business Movement

Preface

The Consultative Business Movement (CBM) was formed in 1988 after lengthy consultation and a ground breaking meeting between 40 senior business leaders and 40 community leaders. When CBM was launched, it aimed to build better understanding between business and the different political and economic actors in South Africa. The first meeting of the CBM's governing body, the National Consultative Group, was held in February 1989.

The principles and values on which CBM was, and is still, based are listed below.

The principles and intentions that unite us are:

☐ building of trust and respect for one another;
☐ creating a representative non-racial democracy;
☐ developing South Africa as one nation for all;
☐ establishing conditions and structures for strong economic growth and just distribution of wealth;
☐ contributing to progress in education, housing, welfare, health and job creation;
☐ increasing consultation with all interest groups;
☐ promoting peace, justice and stability;
☐ achieving full international relations in a post-apartheid society.

In pursuance of all this we:

☐ apply our principles and experience in our own spheres of influence;
☐ consult with all interest groups and democratic movements on an ongoing basis;

☐ interface with the broad base of structures to influence change in support of our principles;
☐ identify and pursue areas of common concern and interest through a process of ongoing consultation;
☐ identify areas of disagreement and conflict and attempt to resolve these through processes of ongoing consultation and debate;
☐ pursue an exploratory and evolutionary transformation role in attempting to arrive at workable solutions for South Africa;
☐ dedicate ourselves to non-partisan consultation with the broadest possible spectrum of interest groups to influence change;
☐ build relationships with various research institutions in order to access reliable information as a basis for the development of strategy and action.

These may seem prosaic, even obvious, to a reader in 1993. In the volatile late 1980s, however, with apartheid still official policy, an ongoing state of emergency and mistrust and antagonism rife, this was a bold and – for many – a dangerous statement.

The CBM, in its first year of existence, essentially played the role of a change agent. It gained its initial credibility as the first (and only) business organisation which existed as the result of an intensive process of consultation between members of the business community and extra-parliamentary organisations, while maintaining its contact with the established parliamentary and business groupings.

CBM's first phase of activities focused on structured contact with political and community groups across the political spectrum. These included the Afrikaner Volkswag, ANC, Azapo, Cosatu, CP, DP, IFP, NP, Nactu and the PAC. Through this process, CBM gained further credibility across the political spectrum as an objective and even-handed organisation, trying to promote the national interest.

A second phase of activity arose out of the need to focus on:

☐ South Africa's macro-economic future;
☐ the role of development in the changing political environment;
☐ the need for 'in-house change', whereby the management of change in companies' organisational culture became consistent with the 'new South Africa'.

These projects drew relevant actors together in structured workshops, and were aimed at facilitating a more mature debate and a better co-ordination of effort in these three areas.

As a consequence of these two phases, CBM was in a favourable position to facilitate multi-lateral discussion on economics, development and peace when these debates began in the broader society.

In the past two years, CBM has become involved in a number of processes, either as a facilitator or providing what can be termed 'process and secretariat services'.

☐ In early 1991 CBM was involved in the process which led to the National Peace Convention and the signing of the National Peace Accord in September of that year. At present, CBM's offices in Natal, the Western Cape and the PWV are either acting as the secretariat to the Regional Dispute Resolution Committees (RDRCs) or are actively involved in Local Dispute Resolution Committees (LDRCs).

☐ At the end of 1991, a range of political parties requested CBM to render process and secretarial services to the Convention for a Democratic South Africa (Codesa). CBM has served in this capacity up to the present time, and is willing to assist in this important task for as long as its expertise is needed.

☐ Towards the end of 1991, CBM was requested to facilitate discussions between organised business and labour on a co-operative mechanism. Since the launch of the National Economic Forum in October 1992, CBM has been acting as its interim secretariat. At regional levels, CBM's offices in the PWV, Natal and the Western Cape are also acting as facilitating secretariats for the Regional Economic Forums in the PWV and Natal, and fulfiling the same role for sub-committees of the Western Cape Regional Economic Forum.

In addition to its role in these forums as a process facilitator and catalyst, CBM has focused on the way in which its members (at present 105 corporations) and the broader business community interact with their environment and deal with their corporate culture and internal business practices. Many business leaders recognised that the role of business needed to be re-examined as part of the broader process of social transition. With this in mind, subsequent CBM initiatives have focused on equal opportunity and equalising opportunity, technical skills training, participative management, and social investment, sensitisation and affirmative action programmes, to name but a few areas of activity.

Acknowledging the importance of these issues, CBM embarked on a process to assist its members in these areas through providing guidelines on in-house change and effective ways of responding to the rapidly changing external environment. This resulted in the 1991 publication of *In-house Change: A Framework and Process for Effective Implementation.*

In further discussions on the role that business should play in the transition, the holistic 'Role of Business in Transition' (RoBiT) approach was conceptualised. The RoBiT programme explores the role of business in this crucial period, and aims to generate options for practical action. This publication is the result of five working sessions, held during 1992, with over 200 business leaders across the country. It aims to provide a framework within which individual businesses can play a constructive role in the transition.

It is hoped that, through the wider distribution of this publication, the CBM will contribute in practical ways to the important role business has to play in the transition.

MANAGING CHANGE

Introduction

Why should business play a role in transition?

Conventional business wisdom of the 1980s held that the 'business of business is business'. However, this view was increasingly challenged by the unconventional macro-environment and, in 1991, Barlow Rand Chairman Mike Rosholt publicly proclaimed that 'the business of business is to stay in business'.

This subtle change of words implied a dramatic departure in thought, strategy and action regarding the mission and vision of business in South Africa.

What brought about this change of heart and vision, and what are its implications for business leaders today?

The inevitability of transition

The view of South Africa's social, economic and political demography from the corporate head offices in the 1980s suggested that society was about to undergo a fundamental and rapid transformation. This was likely to affect the very constitutional, economic and social fabric of South Africa, and entail a complete overhaul of all that business took for granted. Many in business believed that this transformation would be started by a *transition* in political power, inevitably followed by major changes in the economic and social spheres.

Forward looking business leaders had started to ask whether business would survive this transition, and how it should adapt. What forces were shaping the transition? Did the political players understand or care about how business and the economy worked, and how could such understanding be fostered? What would the nature of the transition be, how would business be accommodated in a future constitution and how could business influence the process? And how could business manage the change process so as to minimise disruption, optimise opportunities, create a sound environment for business and achieve economic growth?

The answer to these questions demanded and still demands an overhaul of the everyday operations and machinery of business, from the 'engine room' through to the boardroom. Business faces a challenge to find the right answers, while simultaneously building agreement and co-operation with other stakeholders, both familiar and unfamiliar. An alternative approach to the traditional and hierarchical business decision making process is implicit in this challenge, involving 'new' concepts such as consultation, negotiation and persuasion.

The future of business is at stake

This alternative approach is becoming more important as the transition gathers momentum. While the politicians struggle to reach a political deal, as violence deepens and the economy is paralysed, so the alarm bells for business ring loud. For business leaders in the 1990s, the national interest and the self-interest of business are interwoven and interdependent. This puts the very future of business at stake.

State President PW Botha's plea to business leaders at the 1987 Carlton Conference – 'leave politics to the politicians' and 'get on with the business of business' – is now discredited. Business is not willing or able to trust the future of the economy to any politician, however well-meaning or misguided.

Managing change for survival and growth

In this time of transition, business is called on to generate wealth, consult, manage conflictual relationships, cope with politically motivated action in the economic sphere and mobilise for its own interests. This is largely unfamiliar territory. The folly of disengagement from politics, however, can be measured in strikes, stayaways, violence, failed targets and poor performance. Management of the change process, both internally and externally, is not an extra-curriculum activity. It is a part of the core mission of any business: survival and growth.

The culture and practice of adversarial relationships, bargaining and counter-bargaining which historically characterised management-labour relationships has to be replaced by a new culture and practice of co-determination and consultation. This is as true for the process of nation building as it is for business practices. Any relationship of importance demands mutual respect, integrity, trust and support. The 'bottom line' in both business practices and political-economic negotiations is respectable conduct and level playing fields. Joint ownership of and accountability for decisions and their execution by all stakeholders, and the building of capacity to empower other parties, are important elements of co-determination and change management. These are some of the factors to be taken into account if business and the economy are to be placed on a path of survival and growth.

The apartheid legacy as an impediment to growth and development

We cannot ignore the past when moving into the future, as aspirations feed off past injustices. This is particularly so in South Africa. The high expectations of the disenfranchised loom large for both the politicians who will form the new government, and corporate South Africa. The politicians will look to business to assist in delivery on their promises.

At the same time, business competitiveness increasingly depends on a skilled and productive workforce, sound economic policies, socio-political stability, growing markets and investment. Yet apartheid's legacy has resulted in the exact opposite. The moral poverty of apartheid has resulted in an equivalent poverty of human resource development, mistrust and division. South Africa has to transform itself from a nation which fights within itself to a nation that works together. In this process, business has a crucial role to play.

Laying the foundations for future prosperity

It has almost a truism that no political settlement will be permanent without a sound socio-economic foundation. Future prosperity demands a coherent set of strategies for democracy, peace, growth and development that take account of the inherited legacy of the past, present limitations and future possibilities and aspirations. This is the subject of the complex web of negotiations across many spheres, the outcome of which will determine the shape and workability of a South Africa after transition. Not everything, however, need wait for the completion of multi-party negotiations. Government need not consult before scrapping repressive legislation and business need not wait before investing in productive enterprises. Similarly, programmes of democratisation and reconciliation are urgently required. It is in the enlightened self-interest of corporate South Africa to lay the foundation for future prosperity now, in consultation with other stakeholders.

How can business play a role in transition?

This matter has been the subject of much debate and discussion within the business community, and between business leaders and other interest groups. With this question in mind, CBM convened a series of five workshops entitled 'RoBiT – The Role of Business in Transition' during 1992, dedicated to:

☐ identifying business challenges in the transition;
☐ exploring steps business can take to manage the economic transition in tandem with political transition;
☐ generating options for individual and joint business initiatives.

Over 200 senior business leaders participated in these workshops and this publication is based on their input and discussions. Four distinct aspects of the role of business in the transition were discussed:

☐ the role of business in the broader socio-political environment, including assistance in the birth of a democratic, non-racial constitution and democratic, accountable and sound governance;
☐ the role of business in generating wealth and broadening the management and ownership base of the economy;
☐ the role of the internal practices of business in the change management process and the development of its own structures, functioning and personnel;
☐ the role of business in interfacing with the surrounding communities, fostering peace and development.

Assisting business to play its role in transition

The RoBiT vision is based on a broad acceptance amongst senior business leaders that South African business should contribute, in partnership with all other interest groups, to democracy, peace, growth and development and, in so doing, constructively transform South Africa's political economy. Many business leaders also agree that business needs to be assisted in building its capacity to apply these principles, and in creating a broad-based momentum to transform business structures for this purpose.

The four aspects of the role of business in transition set out above should be seen as integrated and interdependent, based on an holistic approach. CBM aims to assist business in these endeavours by:

☐ providing a conceptual framework and vision;
☐ popularising this approach to business' role in transition;
☐ developing networks and support on a national and regional level;
☐ consulting and interacting with all relevant interest groups;
☐ identifying, pursuing and implementing specific projects;
☐ providing information;
☐ assisting companies, where requested, with their initiatives.

The fundamental point of departure for the RoBiT programme is the need for consultation with all stakeholders, thereby ensuring an inclusive process of joint decision making and responsibility for implementation. The process also requires that the capacity of other stakeholders be built. The RoBiT programme exists as a contribution amongst other existing initiatives, aimed at supporting the role of business in transition. It is, therefore, intended to support and dovetail with, rather than duplicate, existing initiatives.

The key ingredients for the success of the RoBiT strategy are the commitment, involvement and guidance of major economic decision makers, specifically business. These are the foundations that implementation of these concepts will rest on (see diagram 1).

Areas in which business should play a role

The role of business in the macro-environment

The outcome of the transition will depend primarily on the statesmanship and leadership displayed by political leaders across the spectrum. However, business cannot afford to leave the shaping of the macro-environment to political players. The fragility of the political process and the state of the economy demand that business uses its influence appropriately in both the political and economic terrains. Key areas for business influence are identified in Chapter One.

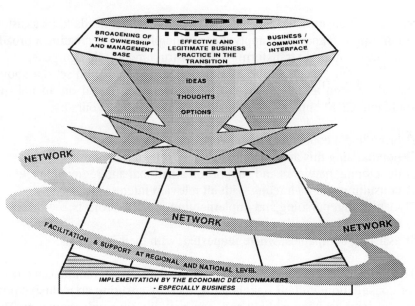

Diagram 1

Broadening the ownership and management base

With eventual political democratisation, most South Africans will expect economic democratisation. Business is, in this context, being increasingly challenged to empower the black community economically by pro-actively broadening the ownership and management base. This aims to give black South Africans a real stake in the economy. The context and options for broadening the ownership and management base are the subject of Chapter Two.

Effective and legitimate business practice in transition

Many business leaders recognise that the transition demands the re-examination of in-company business practices. Changes in business practice will have to answer the question, 'what is in it for me?', posed by both management and the workforce. Chapter Three suggests a framework and practical ideas for effective and legitimate in-company change. In identifying and discussing ten key areas, the emphasis is placed on a committed and integrated approach that has to be completely aligned with company strategy.

The business-community interface

The final chapter is based on the premise that a stable environment for both the future and economic growth will depend on curbing violence, crime and poverty. It emphasises the key role business needs to play in addressing these problems. Already this role is not insignificant, but a greater private sector vision and policy framework is still needed. Chapter Four offers guidelines for a private sector role in peace and development.

A 'manual' for use by individuals, business leaders, corporations and private sector institutions

This publication has been structured to facilitate easy access to information on the subjects covered. Chapters contain:

☐ a framework and context for approaching the issue;
☐ practical options open to business;
☐ case studies of what has been done and achieved by business organisations applying these principles and this framework.

There are many simple steps to be taken by business in meeting the challenges of the transition. The first step is no doubt to analyse the specific problem areas before deciding on a general approach and specific action. Consultation and discussion with interested parties should be part of generating this analysis and strategy.

Networking

All of the RoBiT discussion sessions with business leaders identified the importance of *networking*. This applies not only to different sections within an organisation, but also between different organisations. This has many advantages, one of which is to ensure that effort is not duplicated and resources wasted.

Networking also contributes to informed decision making. A number of possible objectives for the establishment of a network can be put forward:

☐ to ensure effective flow of information on specific relevant topics/ issues;
☐ to facilitate the sharing of ideas and thoughts;

☐ to facilitate discussion of key areas;
☐ to allow people the opportunity for exposure to differing ideas, thoughts and perceptions which can enhance understanding of specific issues;
☐ to allow the opportunity for debate which may lead to specific action plans to address such issues.

In considering the establishment of a network, three prerequisites need to be satisfied:

☐ the purpose of the network requires clear definition in terms of an identified need and the target of the network;
☐ activities forming the basis of the network need to be identified;
☐ the content areas of the intended network need to be clarified.

In conclusion

The material presented here is not exhaustive. To make it more accessible, each chapter has a synopsis or summary, giving the reader a brief overview of the material.

The appendices are designed to assist in identifying resources that can support the further development of ideas. Practically, these resources include regional and national RoBiT committees to assist business and CBM contact people.

It is hoped that economic decision makers will use the perspectives in this book and find them a useful contribution to the debate on the role of business in the transition and beyond. Success will be measured by visible contributions to the mission of democracy, peace, growth and development.

The macro-environment in transition

The inevitability of transition from apartheid to democracy has gradually dawned on South Africans, who now face – for the first time – a non-racial general election.

The outcome of this transition process remains uncertain, with instability, endemic poverty and political conflict rife. On the horizon, though, is the promise of stability, democracy, investment and growth. Whether this promise can be fulfilled will depend, to a large extent, on the statesmanship and leadership of political representatives across the spectrum in rapidly concluding constitutional negotiations.

Business as a key stakeholder in this future can no longer afford to leave the shaping of the macro-environment entirely to political players. The fragile nature of the political process and the state of the economy impel business to assert both its interests and the interests of ordinary South Africans who desire peace and prosperity.

This chapter examines the impact of the macro-environment on business and the role that it needs to play in ensuring that the environment is conducive to growth and development.

The end of 1991 was marked by the historic signing of the Declaration of Intent at Codesa 1. Expectations were high that an interim government and South Africa's first free and fair election would soon follow. The reality was very different, and South Africa was plunged into political and economic stalemate, with commentators describing 1992 as a wasted year.

South Africa cannot afford to squander more time. As politicians endeavour to address outstanding obstacles to peace and a negotiated political settlement, business needs to use its influence to ensure positive outcomes.

There are a number of obstacles to this positive outcome, including issues associated with regional powers, the role of security forces and the civil service, and the holding of free and fair elections. Assisting in the formation and working of a transitional executive structure to prepare for a free and fair election and interim government is an immediate task.

A non-racial government elected in terms of a new democratic constitution is inevitable. What is uncertain, though, is whether the process leading to this will keep all major players on board. If the constitutional process is not widely accepted, it is likely to lead to protracted instability, civil war and repression, accompanied by stagnant or falling economic growth rates, increased crime, social upheaval and hopelessness.

In this context, business needs to focus its efforts on ensuring that economic and socio-economic negotiations deliver tangible results. Ways need to be found of ensuring that government, political players and organised labour effectively co-operate with business in developing strategies for the economic growth, stability and development required to sustain a political settlement. This is a key economic and political challenge.

Chapter One

The macro-environment in transition

The inevitability of transition

The process of change marked by State President FW de Klerk's opening address to parliament on 2 February 1990 has gradually forced most South Africans – who face their first non-racial general election within 12 months – to confront the inevitability of transition.

The key challenge posed by the transition is to lay the foundations for a new South Africa which enjoys stability and progress on the social, political and economic fronts.

The promise offered by this outcome is dimmed by the current reality of instability, endemic poverty and political conflict. Yet future stability, democracy, investment and growth are not unattainable. The efforts made in this phase of transition will determine whether this can be achieved.

Statesmanship and leadership by political figures across the spectrum is crucial if the desired outcome is to have any chance of realisation. It is increasingly apparent, however, that this will also depend on the role that business and other elements of civil society play in assisting these leaders to find a resolution to the current impasse. While the overall process of constitutional negotiations is the responsibility of politicians, business needs to be aware of those areas where its influence and leadership could be of assistance.

Political transition

The realisation of two goals is required to place South Africa on a firm constitutional and political course:

☐ effective transitional (ie interim government) measures to manage the transition; and

☐ ultimately, a government that meets with the approval of a substantial proportion of South Africans.

Diagram 1 outlines the likely process and course of events in South Africa's political transition. The creation of a transitional executive structure, which will prepare the way for a free and fair election and act as the first phase of interim government, is a key first step in this process. This will lead to an elected non-racial interim government responsible for drafting a new constitution. A fully-fledged new government will only be elected once the new constitution is agreed to.

THE FOUR STAGES OF NATIONAL POLITICAL NEGOTIATIONS

STAGE 1. PRE-INTERIM PHASE	PRESENT GOVERNMENT RULES WHILE CODESA III AGREES TO MECHANISMS OF A NATIONAL CONSTITUTION MAKING BODY
STAGE 2. FIRST INTERIM PHASE	TRANSITIONAL EXECUTIVE COUNCIL EXECUTIVE POWERS OVER MATTERS AFFECTING THE LEVELLING OF THE PLAYING FIELDS FOR FREE AND FAIR ELECTIONS. ALL OTHER MATTERS DEALT WITH BY TRICAMERAL PARLIAMENT REGIONAL / LOCAL GOVERNMENT * FIVE SUB COUNCILS FINANCE LAW AND ORDER / SECURITY DEFENCE FOREIGN AFFAIRS ELECTIONS

⟨VIOLENCE⟩

FREE AND FAIR ELECTIONS

STAGE 3. SECOND INTERIM PHASE	FULL INTERIM GOVERNMENT PRIMARY TASK - THE CREATION OF A NEW CONSTITUTION

FREE AND FAIR ELECTIONS

STAGE 4. NEW GOVT.	FULLY FLEDGED DEMOCRATIC GOVERNMENT

Diagram 1

Diagram 2 highlights potential obstacles to peace and a negotiated settlement during the course of constitutional negotiations. The way in which negotiators deal with these obstacles will be critical.

Codesa participants identified two phases of interim government:

☐ the first phase envisages the creation of a Transitional Executive Structure (TEC) to prepare the way for free and fair elections, while the

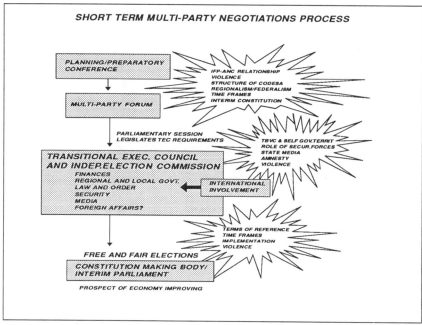

Diagram 2

present governing structures continue to govern over other matters. Sub-councils on regional and local government, finance, law and order, security, defence and foreign affairs are envisaged, as are independent electoral and media commissions with the express purpose of 'levelling the playing fields';

☐ the second phase envisages the election of an interim parliament based on proportional representation which will both draw up the new constitution (via a national assembly) and assume responsibility for governance (via a legislative assembly and interim cabinet).

These phases of interim government are detailed in diagrams 3 and 4. Diagram 5 illustrates the ANC, IFP and NP's preferences for constitutional development. It highlights differences which remain on time frames for the interim government phase and the process of constitution making.

While tremendous progress has been made in negotiations, violence, mass action and the debate on the role of regions and devolution of powers continue to be potential sources of delay for a peaceful and stable transition. The manner in which these issues are resolved will determine the time frame within which free and fair elections could be held.

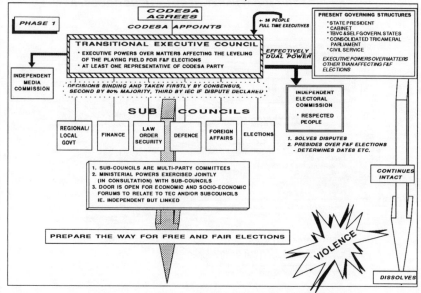

THE TWO PHASES OF INTERIM GOVERNMENT AS PROPOSED AT CODESA 2, MAY 1992

Diagram 3

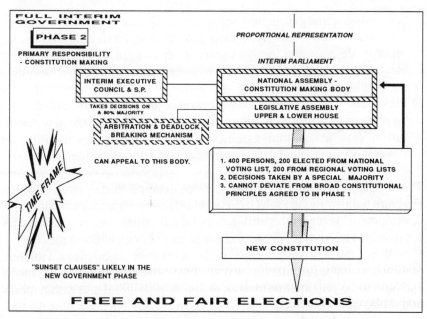

Diagram 4

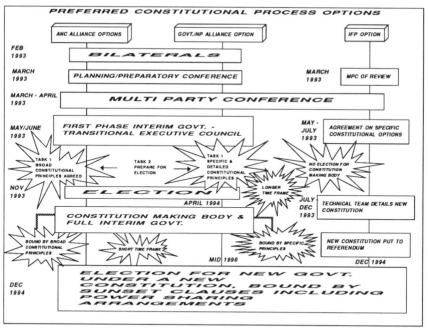

Diagram 5

Violence

Political violence since February 1990 has proved to be a major stumbling block in negotiations and does not augur well for the transition. The National Peace Accord provides important ground rules aimed at limiting political violence, yet as diagram 6 indicates, political violence has remained at extremely high levels.

Violence feeds not only on poverty and crime, but also on a lack of trust and deteriorating relationships between political actors which could plague South Africa well beyond a political settlement. These conflictual relationships are not only the result of poor relationships between individuals, but involve deep and conflicting vested interests.

True commitment to peace will only emerge when political leaders recognise that the cost of conflict and violence exceeds its benefits. Stability is likely to remain a distant hope until such time as a political agreement, which accommodates as far as possible the interests of the major players, is reached.

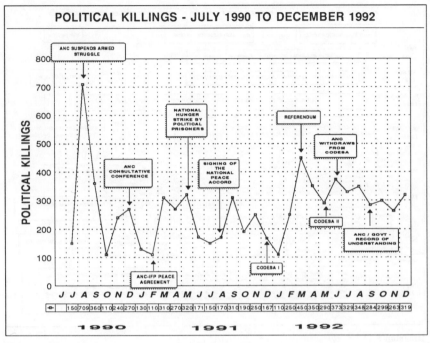

Diagram 6

Regionalism

The role and powers of regions in a future constitution is highly controversial. This issue lay at the heart of the Codesa 2 deadlock and may again be the cause of breakdowns in constitutional talks.

A stormy debate on the appropriateness of regional autonomy, unitary or federal forms of state, and the legitimacy of self-determination can be expected. This will test the limits of the compromises that the negotiating parties are prepared to entertain. Questions over the reincorporation of the nominally independent homeland states (Transkei, Bophuthatswana, Venda and Ciskei) into South Africa, the role of the self-governing territories and their command over resources (including land rights and fiscal autonomy) could all become breakpoints in negotiations. The outcome of these issues and the manner in which it is arrived at will deeply influence the shape of a future South Africa. It is important to introduce the needs of business, the economy and sound governance into the discussion of these issues in order to avoid a wholly ideologically driven debate.

Security forces and the civil service

The role of security forces and the civil service in securing a stable transition cannot be underestimated. A peaceful transition is unlikely to occur unless the security forces and the civil service are harnessed to play a constructive role. Many believe that a pact drawing together the disparate militia, homeland security forces and South African security agencies is a precondition for the transformation of the security forces into legitimate and credible agents for change.

Many civil servants may be more committed to maintenance of past privilege, future job security and pensions than administration of a new transitional arrangement. Yet for both the security forces and the civil service, guarantees of future security without recrimination for past actions, together with a clear policy direction, may be a precondition for their support of transition and a new government.

Electioneering and negotiating simultaneously

The strategy of electioneering and negotiating simultaneously shows a lack of dedication to protecting and nurturing the process of negotiations, as distinct from its outcome. South Africa's leaders have yet to prove their ability to rise above their own narrow interests. This places the entire political process in jeopardy. Pressure by civil society, including business, on the politicians to keep the political process on track will help to make politicians accountable for their actions.

Economic civil war

If the economy, rather than being strengthened by all who have a common interest in survival and prosperity, is used as a political battleground, the potential to move successfully through transition will be jeopardised. This is a major economic challenge to business and other key stakeholders in society.

South Africa's first free and fair election

Within 12 months South Africa is likely to experience its first non-racial general election ever. This is a daunting prospect. The 1992 Angolan election debacle looms large as a scenario to be avoided at all costs. South Africans have never experienced a democratic election and the stakes are particularly high for political parties which have never previously tested

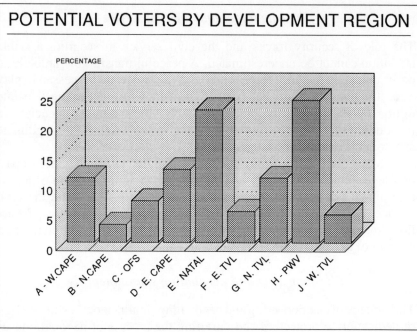

Diagram 7

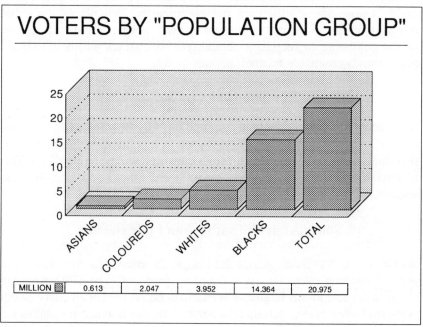

Diagram 8

their popular support in an election. The establishment of an Independent Electoral Commission – a structure proposed at Codesa 2 – which can maintain and monitor the impartiality and fairness of the elections, is crucial.

Besides the role that business can play in this Independent Electoral Commission, it also has a function in voter education programmes. Diagrams 7 and 8 indicate that over 68% of future voters will be participating in an election for the first time in their lives. Many voters will be illiterate and even more will be unsure of the procedures and principles of voting. Many future voters live in rural areas relatively isolated from information on the procedures and importance of voting. Voter education of employees could be a significant contribution by the business sector to a free and fair election.

Economic transition

South Africans are familiar with the refrain that unless a political solution is accompanied by economic growth, any settlement will be a fragile one. The enormity of the challenges facing economic stakeholders is clear in

---

THE ECONOMY: 1992

A SNAPSHOT

LIVING STANDARDS	1966 - R 3 331	
(GDP PER CAPITA)	1992 - R 3 340	

ECONOMIC GROWTH
- NEGATIVE 1,5% GROWTH (1992) FOR THE THIRD YEAR
- DEVELOPING COUNTRIES GROWING AT 3 TO 6%, WITH THE EXCEPTION OF SOUTHERN AND EASTERN AFRICA

UNEMPLOYMENT LEVELS OF ECONOMICALLY ACTIVE POPULATION - 43%

RETRENCHMENTS - STEEL AND ENGINEERING - 25 000 JOBS LOST DURING JANUARY TO SEPT 1992

LABOUR PRODUCTIVITY		
	RSA	18,7% ADVANCE
	GERMANY	33,8%
	USA	55,0%
	JAPAN	120%

LABOUR COST	SOUTH AFRICA	42% HIGHER THAN GERMANY
		58% HIGHER THAN AUSTRALIA
		172% HIGHER THAN SINGAPORE

EXPORTS - RISEN FROM 13,2 (1991) TO 22,6 PERCENT OF GDP

GOVT EXPENDITURE
- REVENUE UNDERSHOOT EXPENDITURE BY R 28 BILLION
- BUDGET DEFICIT 8% OF GDP

Diagram 9

---

the light of some key economic statistics set out in diagram 9. These indicate the extremely fragile condition of the economy. The potential for irrevocable decay and a wasteland scenario looms ever larger.

However, it appears that the economic reality is beginning to dawn on the players and there is a growing convergence of views on economic priorities.

Societies in transition are commonly dominated by political and constitutional issues, with economic issues and the creation of foundations for society post-transition largely relegated to the back-burner. By contrast, the fact that economic issues do feature on South Africa's transitional agenda is a distinctive positive feature.

Since February 1990, players have moved from debating economic issues in workshops and conferences to formalising mechanisms for addressing economic matters. This is seen in multilateral economic and socio-economic forums at national, regional and sectoral levels. Participants believe that these forums can address immediate priorities at the same time as charting longer term strategies.

This development is to be welcomed and encouraged. It is in part a result of a strong and well organised trade union movement, as well as a private sector that is increasingly active in the broader socio-economic and political environment. These two major stakeholders, as well as government and other players, are propagating the view that economic policy formulation is not the preserve of government. All economic stakeholders have a role.

This view of economic policy formulation recognises that a co-operative approach is probably the only way to address the current economic decay.

The political impasse of the early 1990s saw the economy turned into a political battleground. Boycotts, strikes and stayaways on the one hand, and retrenchments and wage cuts on the other, became constant features of the economic landscape. Players lost the vision and will to place the economy above sectional interests. Co-operation and joint problem solving is thus a first critical step to economic progress during transition.

Co-operative processes: mechanisms for an economy in transition

During 1991 and 1992, many interest groups argued that the economic challenge could not be put on hold pending a political settlement. Co-operative mechanisms were needed to focus on both immediate and long term economic development and growth needs. These mechanisms are geared to creating a better understanding and possibility of co-operation in the development and implementation of economic policy, at the same time as the constitutional process and new government structures unfold.

The economic and socio-economic arena is now characterised by a multitude of such mechanisms, as set out in diagram 10. These include:

☐ the National Economic Forum (NEF);
☐ Regional Economic and Development Forums which are either opera-tive or are being planned in each of the existing development regions;
☐ the National Housing Forum (NHF), launched on 31 August 1992;
☐ a tripartite taskforce in the textile industry, working on a strategy for this ailing economic sector;
☐ a National Consultative Forum on Drought, launched in June 1992.

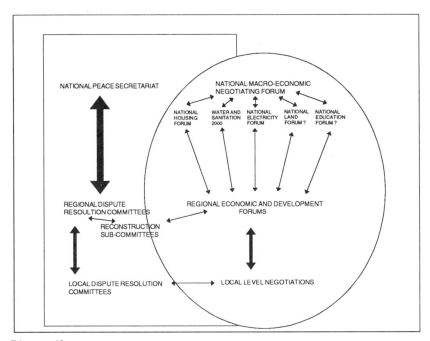

Diagram 10

It is a key challenge for all stakeholders, business included, to ensure that these processes and structures succeed in tackling substantive issues. If these mechanisms do not deliver tangible results, they could contribute to South Africa's long list of problems rather than alleviating them.

The state of the economy: a statistical snapshot

Some of the key economic statistics set out in diagram 9 clearly demonstrate the enormity of the challenges facing economic stakeholders. Crucial indicators include the following:

Recession

South Africa has experienced its worst recession since the beginning of the century. The business cycle turned in late 1989, taking the economy even more firmly into the grip of recession.

Structural distortions

The recession is accompanied by deep structural distortions, which are at the core of the country's economic problems. These include economic inefficiencies, social and economic inequalities, as well as areas of underdevelopment and poverty.

Living standards

Finance Week estimates that real GDP per capita in 1992 was R3 340, comparable to the 1966 figure of R3 331 (*Finance Week*, 24-30 September 1992).

Economic growth

South Africa's record of economic growth over the decade 1982 to 1992 was amongst the worst in the world. The average annual real GDP increase for the period 1982/92 was 0,7 per cent. It is estimated that real GDP for 1992 was -1,5 per cent, taking South Africa into its third year of negative growth (South African Reserve Bank quarterly bulletin, September 1992).

Unemployment

Forty-three per cent of the economically active population is unemployed. While the formal sector was able to absorb 81 per cent of all new labour market entrants during the 1960s, by 1991 this figure had fallen to just seven per cent (Standard Bank Economic Review, September 1992)

Retrenchments

Retrenchments continue at a high level. In the steel and engineering industry, for example, retrenchments totalled 13 800 in the first five months of 1992, up 27 per cent on the same period in 1991. By September 1992 the figure had risen to 25 000 (Seifsa statistics, October 1992).

Fixed investments

The Reserve Bank states that net domestic investments as a portion of GDP declined to one per cent in the second quarter of 1992, compared with average ratios of 14 per cent in the 1970s and eight per cent in the 1980s (South African Reserve Bank quarterly bulletin, September 1992).

It is of grave concern that more and more of an already inadequate proportion of resources going into fixed investment is utilised to replace or repair existing investment.

Business confidence

In its manufacturing survey for the third quarter of 1992, Stellenbosch University's Bureau for Economic Research claimed that business conditions and confidence were on a level comparable to the third quarter of 1985 – a particularly low point.

Capital outflows

The Reserve Bank points to a R1,9 billion net capital outflow in the second quarter of 1992 (South African Reserve Bank quarterly bulletin, September 1992).

Development status

Table 1 below sets out the results of a 1990 World Bank survey comparing South Africa's development status to that of other countries.

Table 1:

Low income countries	Lower middle income	South Africa	Upper middle income	Industrial market economies
Per capita income (US dollars)				
290	1 200	1 800	2 710	14 670
Manufacturing share in GDP (percentage)				
12	17	23	25	30
Life expectancy at birth (years)				
61	64	60	68	76
Infant mortality rate (per 1 000 infants under one year old)				
76	61	72	50	9
Level of urbanisation (percentage)				
30	51	57	66	77

Source: World Bank, 1990

Housing

The De Loor task group has suggested that 198 000 houses need to be built each year for the next ten years to eliminate housing backlogs. In 1990, the task group estimated that the housing backlog in the urban areas of South Africa (including urban areas in the ten homelands) was 1,3 million units. The task group noted that information on housing backlogs in rural areas was not available, but added that a large proportion of the houses of the 3,1 million families living in rural areas in 1990 needed upgrading. *Engineering News* estimated in February 1992 that 1 300 new houses had to be built every day for the next ten years to overcome the housing crisis.

Education

South Africa's education and skills crisis continues, as indicated in tables 2 and 3 below.

Table 2:

Claimed levels of education among African adults aged 16 and over (as %)		
	1985	1989/90
No school	22	24
Some primary	32	32
Primary completed	12	10
Some high	28	27
High completed	5	5
Some post matric	2	2

Source: South Institute of Race Relations, *Race Relations Survey*, 1992.

Table 3:

Literate adults in South Africa, 1985 (Percentage of population over 13 who have 5 or more years of formal education)			
	Urban	Rural	Total
Black	70.1	37.9	53.1
Coloured	85.1	44.1	73.4
Asian	85.6	74.5	84.8
White	98.5	97.9	98.4

Source: South African Institute of Race Relations, *Race Relations Survey*, 1992.

Drought

Drought in 1992 ravaged rural communities and the agricultural sector, contributing 1,8 per cent to the shrinking of South Africa's economy.

Government revenue and expenditure

Government revenue in 1992 could undershoot expenditure by at least R28 billion. This implies a budget deficit of approximately eight per cent of GDP. The government interest burden in terms of public debt occupies the second largest place in terms of government expenditure items. It is preceded only by expenditure on education. Of concern is that government expenditure is concentrated on current and not capital expenditure.

World economic downturn and commodity prices

These factors impacted negatively on economic performance. An upturn was forecast for 1993, but Finance Minister Keys projected a South African lag of nine months.

On balance

There are some positive indicators. For example, inflation is less worrying than before, and exports have picked up. While in 1984 exports as a percentage of GDP were 13,2 per cent, by 1991 this figure had risen to 22,6 per cent (*Finance Week*, 24-30 September 1992).

On balance, however, commentators warn of the prospects of irrevocable decay unless bold steps are taken to address the South African economic situation.

The economy: a political battlefield

This frightening economic reality is beginning to dawn on the players, yet recurring efforts are bedeviled by delays in the political process. The launch of the National Economic Forum (NEF) in 1992, for instance, was delayed as a result of breakdowns caused by political deadlocks. Economic development is being used by political players as a mechanism for winning votes.

Against a stark background of negative economic growth and deepening poverty, the responsibility of all stakeholders, politicians included, must be to create the conditions for economic recovery.

There is no shortage of economic policy perspectives on requirements to place the economy on a path of sustained growth and development. These have emerged from across the spectrum. There is also a growing convergence amongst players on economic priorities. Co-operation between the players in realising these priorities will be crucial in determining whether South Africa grows and prospers in the future or whether the wasteland scenario becomes a reality. All stakeholders share this responsibility.

Most analysts agree that the introduction of political democratisation in the context of poverty and poor economic performance is one of South Africa's key difficulties. Equally, the nature of constitutional choices will have implications for the ability of a future government to address social and economic imbalances, and create the conditions for stability, investment and growth. South Africans wish not only for the vote, but for shelter, food and jobs. While a political settlement is an essential condition for this economic recovery, putting the economy on a solid foundation in the interim needs to be given top priority.

Positive indicators in the macro-environment

South African political leaders have managed to rise above their enormous political differences in an effort to end violence. The greater consensus regarding the principles underlying the constitution making body and the need for power sharing in and beyond the interim government phase is also a positive recent development.

The varied and multi-levelled negotiations occurring around peace, economics and social development is a further positive indicator. The focus on peace by national political leaders indicates an acceptance that freedom of political expression and association, and implementation of strategies to end violence, are necessary parts of successful negotiations.

The various transitional forums are designed to facilitate development during the transition. These new forums also provide the foundation for future inclusive mechanisms to develop and implement policy after the election of a new government. In particular, the NEF provides hope that future economic policy will build on current consensus.

The role of the international community and its willingness to assist, is yet another positive sign that the transition can be managed. In particular, its role in observing the peace process and in monitoring a free and fair election is important.

Implications of the macro-environment for business

The primary task of business is wealth creation and investment in a future South Africa. This requires an environment conducive to business.

Business can no longer afford to leave the shaping of the macro-environment to political parties and government. The fragile nature of the constitutional negotiations, the potential stumbling blocks outlined earlier and the state of the economy demand that business organises to assert its interests and the interests of millions of ordinary South Africans who desire peace and prosperity.

Business will need to exercise leadership and influence to ensure that the transition proceeds smoothly and rapidly.

Business itself has enormous potential to impact positively on the macro-scenario. The development of scenarios such as the Old Mutual/Nedcor one, and the emphasis on strategic planning that has emerged in the private sector over the last few years, places business in a position to understand the practical challenges facing South Africa, and to share an informed perspective with other players.

Business is increasingly acting together with other civil society groups in order to influence political and economic developments. The Saccola-Cosatu initiative prior to the 3 August 1992 stayaway was an important indication of this. It arose from an understanding that if business, labour and churches could act together on the basis of common values and a common interest in a peaceful negotiated settlement, this would be a powerful pressure on the political parties to cease jockeying for power and act in the national interest. These civil society partners attempted to refocus the political parties on the way back to negotiations.

While the parties to the Saccola-Cosatu charter could not agree on a proposed one-day shutdown, they did, to a large extent, agree on the content of the charter. Co-operation between business, labour and churches may in the future provide a powerful basis for influencing the macro-political scenario.

Business can in these ways choose to use its *legitimate and powerful* influence more directly to pursue a rapid and democratic settlement.

Business has open lines created through years of dedicated consultation and networking. It needs to use these lines of communication to facilitate sensible debate on the major issues of the day. This role requires:

☐ solid information and well thought out policy options which can be rapidly accessed;

- [ ] an easily accessible network of people close to the pulse of decision making and a feel for the process;
- [ ] trust and openness of the parties toward business and acceptance of business' possible role;
- [ ] knowing when to act and when not to act.

The peace process and National Economic Forum are good examples of how business has co-operated with other stakeholders and can continue to meet particular objectives. In particular,

- [ ] the business community – as one major stakeholder – has a responsibility to ensure that it does not allow politics to obscure important economic challenges. It also needs to examine how it can use its leverage to lobby other stakeholders to create the conditions for economic recovery and growth;
- [ ] business should help ensure that forums focus on substantive discussions and deliver tangible results;
- [ ] business should inject a vision of how South Africa could be a prosperous and democratic nation, and propose strategies to achieve this.

Conclusion

A best case, short term, outlook seems to be the formation of a Transitional Executive Council (TEC) before mid-1993, leading to an election in December 1993. However, many opinion makers have commented that unless there are dramatic developments the process is likely to drag out a lot longer.

Whatever the case, economic conditions cannot afford further delays in the political process. These could lead the international community to write off South Africa as yet another hopeless 'basket case' country unable to deal with its own problems.

Two feasible constitutional scenarios (see diagram 11 opposite) can be realistically identified. The *'negative outcome'* scenario envisages a breakdown in consensus between some parties on the constitution making process. In this scenario, violence (from those who perceive they have been excluded from the constitutional process) accompanied by repression (by the TEC participants aimed at countering this violence) bedevils South Africa's first election for an interim government. This leads ultimately to a new government which is severely limited by instability, hopelessness and powerful opposition groups. This leads by 1997 to economic and social disaster and a crisis of governance.

On the other hand the *'positive outcome'* scenario envisages agreement on the constitution making process, even if there are tensions and delays regarding the interim constitution and the detail of constitutional principles. Even under this scenario of structured elections for a Constitution Making Body, economic growth in 1993 and 1994 is likely to be below the level of population growth (2,5%). This reality will be accompanied by limited capacity of the interim government to stem violence and instability. Under these conditions foreign investment will also be limited. While under this scenario a full interim government governs in 1995 and 1996, and real economic growth and stability begin to be possible, social pressures and low living standards will still be realities. By 1997 under this scenario it could be possible to achieve political stability and economic growth (3-5%) to put South Africa on to the high road.

Even then, according to economist Servaas van der Bergh, optimistic projections of 3% per annum employment growth and GDP growth rates of 6% per annum would still leave seven million people unemployed at

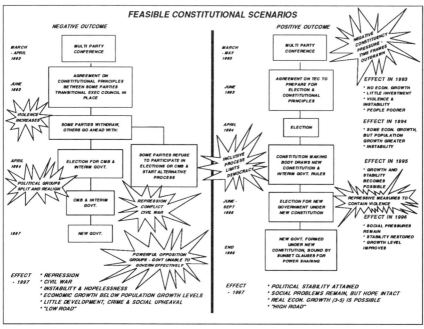

Diagram 11

the turn of the century. This will be a tremendous political and social burden reflective of the deep social demands which will still exist.

There can be no doubt that the next four years could be some of the most testing for South Africans in general, and business people in particular. The dramatic quality and pace of change will place intense pressure on the environment in which business is done. The effect, not only on the macro-political and economic environment, but on the workforce and all other South Africans, will be enormous. Under these conditions, productivity and growth will be goals as difficult to meet as they will be important.

For this reason special strategies and efforts will be required for business to keep a pace with these changes. Those who are pro-active stand to survive and grow, while those who fold their arms and hope the problem goes away may find themselves left in the wilderness.

2

Broadening the ownership and management base

Increasingly, business is being called on to empower the black community economically. The challenge for business is to build, in a pro-active way, a real stake in the economy amongst the black community by broadening the ownership and management base of the economy.

What, in terms of reality, expectations and perceptions, lies behind this challenge, and how can business respond? The current reality is that the black community has a very limited stake in the economy. Black people own little of the country's wealth. Those who run their own businesses are largely located in the informal sector. The formal sector has a dearth of black directors and managers. Only five per cent of managerial jobs are occupied by blacks. Studies suggest that, by the year 2000, South Africa will need an additional 120 000 higher level managers, with whites only able to fill 45 000 of these positions. Black economic empowerment is not only a social responsibility, but also an imperative for economic growth.

The gap between reality and the expectations of the disenfranchised is well known. It is in this context that calls for redistribution are heard, ringing alarm bells within business. Yet such calls often have more to do with a desire for democratisation of the economy and the broadening of opportunities for effective black participation than redistribution in and of itself.

Within the black community, decades of exclusion and negative experiences of the South African economic system have resulted in deep suspicion and criticism of what exists. When business calls for workers to be more productive and contribute to company economic performance, it is important to acknowledge that negative responses are often the result of an expectation of little real return. Exclusion has also resulted in low levels of economic and business literacy, making effective participation difficult.

Against this background of reality, expectations, perceptions and real need, the call for business to broaden its ownership and management base is both justified and in the interests of growth.

There are a wide range of practical options through which business can respond to this situation. The process of broadening the ownership and management base ranges on a continuum from equity ownership in the form of holdings in equity and risk capital and financial control, to participation in management processes.

Ownership possibilities range from ownership in the formal sector, through small and medium sized enterprises (SMEs), to the informal sector. Ownership through participation in management processes ranges from collective participation in decision making to individual participation in the ranks of management.

Broadening the ownership base essentially covers two mutually inclusive areas, namely the mobilisation of capital to facilitate involvement, and specific efforts to ensure effective involvement. There are numerous existing and planned initiatives to address the first issue, including the creation of a South African Development Trust and the Community Growth Fund (CGF), an investment fund launched by major trade unions. This former initiative includes the development of SMEs, assistance to the informal sector and sub-contracting.

Options for addressing the broadening of the management base include setting company targets, extending company training facilities to SMEs and the informal sector, and management apprenticeship schemes. Importantly, local and international affirmative action programmes highlight a number of important lessons to be learnt in addressing this issue.

The context and options for broadening the ownership and management base in the South African economy are the subjects of this chapter.

Chapter Two

Broadening the ownership and management base

Once South Africa achieves a political settlement, the new government will no doubt look to the economy to service its needs, policies and support base. If business is to counter short and long term destructive economic policy, it will need to be pro-active in identifying possible demands, challenges and solutions.

The fundamental question posed in this regard is whether established groupings within the economy and business can act with statesmanship to empower the black community economically.

While participative management, development and other initiatives are important, the challenge faced by business is to build a real stake in the economy amongst the black community. Without the ownership base of the economy being broadened, the economy will continue to be viewed as the domain of whites. If this occurs, there will be little incentive for productivity, responsible economic decision making and participation in the economy. Broadening the ownership and management base should be viewed as an important part of placing South Africa on a path of sustained economic growth.

Expectations, perceptions and reality

The current reality

There are important disparities which currently exist in ownership and management. A study for the period 1945-1980 indicated that five per cent of South Africans owned 88 per cent of the wealth (*Economist*, October

1991). By comparison, the top five per cent in United States owns 44 per cent of the economy, and 34 per cent in Germany.

As in other countries, small businesses play an important role in the South African economy. But in South Africa, most small businesses are concentrated in the informal sector.

An analysis of the distribution of business and the number of employees in each of the various sectors of the economy indicates that approximately 70 per cent of businesses operate in the informal sector, which employs approximately 6,3 million people (see diagram 1). This is not, however, an accurate reflection of the extent to which blacks effectively participate in the economy.

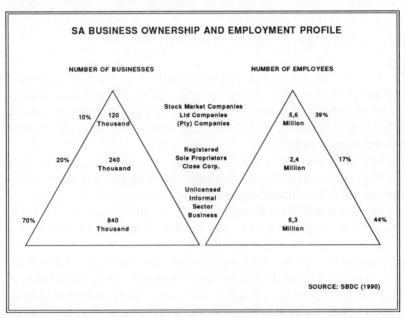

Diagram 1

From another perspective, 66 per cent of businesses in the United States employing less than nine people contribute some 43 per cent to GNP. In South Africa the estimated contribution is 15 per cent.

The informal and small business sector, by no means insignificant in terms of contribution to economic activity, is hamstrung by many constraining factors, such as lack of business skill, capital shortage and over-regulation. This inhibits the even more significant contribution that this sector could make to economic activity.

Management disparities and needs

Various studies indicate that 95 per cent of managerial jobs are presently occupied by whites. South Africa will need an additional 120 000 higher level managers by the year 2000, of which whites will be able to account for 45 000 only. If only on the basis of need, there is a case to be made for the urgent integration of blacks into managerial positions.

Directorships

The shortage of black representatives on corporate boards is cited by Don Mkhwanazi as an indication of the massive imbalances created by apartheid. His preliminary analysis found that, of the top 100 companies listed on the JSE, only two per cent of approximately 2 550 directorships were held by blacks.

In addition, fewer than 30 members of a leading South African corporation's board control over 250 directorships in other companies. As Mkhwanazi argues:

> *Whilst it is true that highly qualified and distinguished individuals of calibre serve on South African boards, it is doubtful that they could apply themselves as effectively as they might wish or as often as their boardroom seats demand. It is my belief that these directors are over-committed and over-stretched.*

Mkhwanazi believes that to achieve an adequate representation of black executive directors, a critical mass of top, senior and middle black managers must be in place (*Indicator SA*, 9(2), Autumn 1992).

Understanding expectations

On the broader macro-economic front, the gap between expectation and reality is well known. The newly enfranchised will expect that political power involves economic power as well. Where reality cannot meet this expectation, realistic or not, of the majority, the government of the day will be placed under extreme pressure to place greater emphasis on delivery for immediate or short term benefit.

Patrick Ncube, an economist in the ANC's Department of Economic Policy, suggested in an interview that:

> *The unemployed want to know what the society we are trying to build will provide for them. One way of dealing with their expectations is*

to look at the needs of the unemployed and lower income categories. These relate to areas like housing, electricity and education. When we build schools and clinics it should be with labour intensive methods and local people should get the job (Die Suid Afrikaan, April/Mei 1992, p27).

Where there is a disjuncture between expectations and reality, redistribution of wealth becomes a burning issue and key cause for concern in business circles and the white community. Very often, though, calls for redistribution have more to do with a desire for democratisation of the economy and the broadening of opportunities for effective black participation in the economy than with redistribution in and of itself.

Jabu Mabuza, Executive President of Fabcos, in a talk delivered at the RoBiT session in Port Elizabeth, summarised the issue of redistribution in the following way:

Black leaders are accordingly calling for a redistribution of wealth – or at least, that is what they seem to be demanding. What they are actually seeking is a restructuring of the economy in order to achieve a fairer distribution of wealth ... If by the mid-1990s, South Africa has a broadly acceptable political settlement, but there has been no change in the distribution of wealth, then it is quite probable that the constitutional arrangements will not hold.

And according to the ANC's Ncube:

Many people misunderstand the ANC when we say that there must be redistribution in South Africa. By redistribution we mean two things. Firstly, it concerns giving resources to those who did not have resources before. When we talk about redistribution we are not talking about handouts, we are talking about democratisation of the economy at various levels. We are talking about reducing unemployment and about supporting the informal sector and small business. This is redistributing sustainable resources.

Ncube further suggested that this second area of redistribution should be from the large urban centres to the rural areas, through which a stake in the economy could be brought to rural dwellers.

At the Carlton Conference in May 1990, hosted by the CBM on the theme of 'Business and the ANC – options for building an economic future', Nelson Mandela made a number of significant statements while expounding the ANC's view of nationalisation and redistribution:

> *Today, I am not going to present any argument about nationalisation. I would however like to share a secret with you. The view that the only words in the economic vocabulary that the ANC knows are nationalisation and redistribution is mistaken. There are many issues we shall have to consider as we discuss the question of democratisation and the deracialisation of economic power ... I am therefore raising the question that the matter of redistribution of wealth in conditions of a growing economy, is one that must be faced squarely and addressed firmly.*

At the same conference Gavin Relly, then executive director of the Anglo American Corporation, stated that:

> *We are united by a vision of South Africa where there is a more equitable distribution of resources ... Meaningful, productive economic opportunities for all South Africans to share in wealth creation ... We in business are dedicated to debate and discussion on the options so that we can build a common economic future.*

Understanding perceptions and experience

In the black community, decades of exclusion and negative experiences of the South African economic system have led to deep suspicion and criticism of the free enterprise system.

Jabu Mabuza of Fabcos puts it this way:

> *The attitude of the black community and black business to the current economic system differs substantially from that of white business. The reason is that the route they had to follow, through the restrictions placed on black business, was via the informal sector. The attitude of the black community is one of deep mistrust and far removed from respect and affection.*

This exclusion has very often resulted in low levels of economic and business literacy. If companies want employees to contribute constructively to economic performance, sharing information and enhancing understanding of economic and business processes is important.

The call for business to be pro-active in the process of black economic empowerment has been raised in many quarters. Against the background of reality, expectations and perceptions, this call seems justified. However, pro-activeness in this area is also critical in placing the South African economy on a path of sustained economic growth.

In the next section, practical options for broadening the ownership and management base are explored.

Practical options for broadening the ownership and management base

A first step in addressing the challenge of broadening the economic ownership and management base involves the development of the concepts being used (see diagram 2).

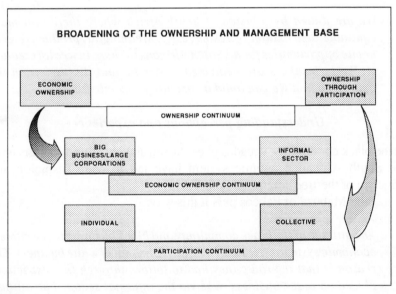

Diagram 2

The concept of ownership ranges on a continuum from economic ownership in the form of holdings in equity and risk capital and financial control, to participation in management processes. Ownership extends over the total spectrum from ownership in the formal sector, small and medium sized enterprises, through to the informal sector.

Ownership through participatory decision making processes in companies forms a further continuum which ranges from collective participation in the decision making process by groups of employees in the area of work, to individual participation in the ranks of management. The majority of workers participate in this area, which therefore lends emphasis to its recognition as an important element in dealing with the total spectrum of the ownership and management base.

From the preceding argument two mutually inclusive areas demand emphasis:

☐ the challenge of broadening the economic ownership base needs to be coupled with the challenge of developing effective management of such enterprises;
☐ for this purpose, it is not only acquisitions and financial resources that count. Training, broadening of the skills base, and enhancing the management culture of the black community are also vital.

In what follows, ownership and management will be addressed separately, although their complementary nature is accepted.

Broadening the ownership base

Numerous *vehicles and options* can be explored when dealing with the challenge of broadening the ownership base. These can make a significant impact not only on perceptions, but also in the area of experienced benefit and tangible economic development. Possibilities arise in both the formal and informal sector.

Broadening the economic ownership base essentially covers two mutually inclusive areas, namely the *mobilisation of capital* to facilitate involvement, and specific efforts to ensure *effective involvement.*

Capital mobilisation: Two of the problems that have to be addressed when examining capital mobilisation involve securing the necessary funds to start or expand a business, and making funds available for blacks to participate in the economy effectively through the ownership of risk capital. There are numerous existing and planned initiatives to address this issue. These include:

☐ a multi-billion dollar package of development assistance which has been considered in the United States. It would cover areas such as the

creation of a South African Development Trust, expanded assistance in black education and the financing and construction of low-cost housing through private sector trusts like the Urban Foundation and the Get Ahead Foundation. Whether some of these initiatives will materialise will be partly dependent on the nature of future economic policies and a willingness to create non-partisan independent vehicles;
□ a proposal to mobilise funds internationally, in order to focus on black economic empowerment and development;
□ a range of support programmes, with priority given to emerging businesses, promotion of black ownership and control in the formal economy, rural development, farmer support and infrastructure;
□ additional support programmes giving priority to education and training, health care, water, sanitation, electricity and the development of management skills and competence;
□ development investments by insurance companies in black communities, in areas such as the financing of businesses; the financing and construction of low-cost housing; the purchasing and development of land for housing; the provision of education and health services; and the financing and construction of industrial premises;
□ the Community Growth Fund (CGF), an investment fund launched by major trade unions, which will deploy a portion of their members' pension and provident fund contributions in 'socially responsible' JSE-listed companies. This, and other avenues of participation through pension and provident fund investments, can effectively bring the disenfranchised into the mainstream of business. Cyril Ramaphosa has argued that the CGF means that workers are no longer spectators in the economy, but active participants in determining their own economic destinies.

Effective involvement in the economy: Development of the small and medium sized sector of the economy is a vital component of broadening the South African economy. Limiting factors to the growth of small and medium sized enterprises (SMEs) include access to capital (largely due to non-qualification for credit in terms of collateral and credit ratings), lack of managerial and business skill, inadequate infrastructure and regulatory constraints.

The benefits inherent in the development of the small and medium business sector should not only be seen in the context of economic stimulation, but also as an area of effective job creation and a training ground for budding young businessmen and women. In the South African context it is necessary to include the informal sector in this category.

There are a number of areas where business can play a facilitating and developmental role in the small and medium business sector:

Informal sector activity: A study conducted by the Get Ahead Foundation highlighted the manner in which informal sector entrepreneurs obtain loans. The study indicated that only nine per cent obtained loans through banks while 70 per cent depended on families and friends for finance (*Business Day*, 19 August 1992).

A Michigan State University survey, conducted on request by the Get Ahead Foundation, found that there are relatively fewer businesses in the extreme top and lower ends of the small enterprise scale. Only 2,8 per cent employ six to ten workers, 0,5 per cent employ between 11 and 50 workers (Get Ahead Foundation Newsletter, November 1991).

Further interesting findings emerging from this research indicated that:

☐ the informal sector produces an average rate of employment growth of 23,9 per cent a year;
☐ the informal sector contributes to more than half of the household income of those households surveyed;
☐ trading is the dominant activity, with manufacturing accounting for only 16,9 per cent. Dressmaking, brewing and shoe repairing are the leaders in this field;
☐ more than half of the informal sector labour force consists of women;
☐ seventy per cent operates from home, typically without any outward sign of activity;
☐ constraints and problems experienced relate to finance, marketing difficulties, government policy, work space or location inadequacies and transport;
☐ almost a fifth of these enterprises started with a business loan;
☐ stokvels generate a large pool of funds (at least 20 per cent of those interviewed were stokvel members).

The informal sector is already making inroads into the formal sector. However, even greater effort is needed to investigate methods and areas whereby the informal sector and SMEs can provide quality products and services to the formal sector.

Relations with SMEs: Business needs to examine its relationship to small and medium enterprises. There is a perception amongst those involved in SMEs that big business does not want them to exist or grow, and that very few big businesses extend a hand of friendship to them.

Sub-contracting: As part of a process of interaction between large enterprises and SMEs, companies could investigate where services could be allocated to sub-contractors and actively search for black small businesses that can cater for these needs. In Natal, for example, a specific directory of black entrepreneurs has been developed.

Where existing small businesses cannot cater for the specific needs of larger companies, one could look at the creation of satellite businesses that are able to do so. This could be done through assisting with finance in the form of minority stakeholding in such a small business, and the provision of full-time managerial and other types of support at the outset.

Ruth Tearl *(Die Suid Afrikaan*, April/Mei 1992, p46) has argued that the area of sub-contracting is expanding. Examples abound in the areas of stationery, printing, manufacturing of roller doors, safety clothing, uniforms, rubber mudguards, reconditioned fridges, office furniture, building materials, reconditioned engines, plants, cleaning materials, bicycles, curtains, linen, computer paper, mining equipment and flowers.

Tearl also highlighted the growing co-operation and, in some instances, joint ventures between the formal sector and SMEs and the informal sector. Examples of this include the following:

☐ the Small Business Development Corporation (SBDC) holds an annual Matchmakers Fair where large business is brought into contact with small business, and the formal sector is encouraged to specify activities/services that they could sub-contract to the small businesses;
☐ the Foundation for African Businesses and Consumer Services (Fabcos), already active in the informal sector of the economy, is involved in a range of initiatives to provide its affiliates with competitive links to the formal sector, for example in retailing, transport, beauty products and catering;
☐ the Get Ahead Foundation provides linkage through initiatives like 'Matchmaking' and a Business Resource Directory (Get Ahead Newsletter, November 1991);
☐ Anglo American and De Beers' Small Business Division, with a turnover of R34 million, has placed sub-contracts with some 130 small businesses.

Broadening of the management base

Broadening the ownership base without supporting it with commensurate capacity building, and providing the necessary skills base to effectively staff organisations, will not only undermine the competitiveness, faith in and support for such organisations, but will also lead to frustration amongst employees.

Why broaden the management base?

There are numerous reasons why business should embark on a process of broadening of the management base. Some of the more obvious include the following:

☐ a new government may well consider imposing race and gender quotas for management positions as a means of satisfying the demand by the electorate for greater participation in the economy. The extent to which business is pro-active will have a bearing on the need, nature and extent of state intervention after the transition from apartheid;
☐ a long range view of the human resource requirements of organisations suggests that the current narrow resource pool will not satisfy the future managerial requirements of companies;
☐ it is vital to enhance and deepen financial and business management skills to ensure an effective broadening of the economic ownership base.

Current practice and perspectives

Programmes to broaden the management base have been undertaken with limited levels of success. These have tended to be targeted at internal company needs and requirements. Reasons for the poor success records of such programmes include:

☐ in some instances such programmes were regarded as window dressing;
☐ a perceived lack of sincerity and commitment;
☐ a lack of constant training, assessment and mentorship;
☐ a lack of attention to the fears of white middle management and the aspirations of black candidates.

It has been argued that affirmative action policies in countries such as the United States, Malaysia and Zimbabwe have been largely unsuccessful. In all instances, these policies were instituted to correct social disparities and benefit a specific group over others.

Social and political lessons both in South Africa and elsewhere suggest a need for pragmatism in approach and implementation. In the United States, after 20 years of affirmative action programmes, opportunities for the truly disadvantaged have deteriorated and only a few privileged blacks have experienced upliftment.

Approaches to broadening the management base

The following guidelines are useful when embarking on practical programmes:

☐ the need to open up opportunities to all, both in recruitment and training;
☐ the need to provide for an equalising component, particularly when assessing educational qualifications, for the previously disenfranchised;
☐ the importance of providing support structures, networks and mentors;
☐ the inequalities created by apartheid extend beyond the economic sector, and affirmative action should embrace the quality of life in its totality;
☐ the process should take cognisance of the fears of whites and the aspirations of blacks. A business acculturation component is essential;
☐ affirmative action should be seen as an interim measure to correct deficiencies, and should have a definite end target date;
☐ self-sufficiency and competitiveness must form key elements of any affirmative action programme. To create a programme based solely on moral principles will lead to numerous problems such as an anti-achievement mentality and a lowering of quality;
☐ it is important to acknowledge perceptions of affirmative action programmes by blacks and their experience of such programmes. There is a strong resistance to being labelled a product of affirmative action. This indicates the importance of being recognised as having gained access and position on the basis of merit and equal opportunity.

With these guidelines as background, there are a number of initiatives that may be considered by individual companies, or as joint initiatives in the business community.

Company targets: Companies should, as part of their strategic plans, build specific targets into their human resource requirements and ensure that the incumbents will be effectively equipped in the workplace through commensurate training and development plans.

Extending training facilities to SMEs and the informal sector: Very often, existing managerial and financial training programmes are not fully utilised, and vacancies could be filled by SME entrepreneurs at minimal or no additional cost. For businesses sub-contracting to SMEs, this could ensure that the relevant SME is staffed by adequately skilled persons.

Second specific full-time personnel to sub-contracted firms: Where an organisation is sub-contracting to a SME in which the organisation has a minority shareholding, it may be advantageous to second a full-time, suitably qualified person to the SME to assist with its establishment and management. This approach will assist the business in its start-up challenge and at the same time enable training and development to take place in the practical environment of the business.

Management apprenticeship programmes: The objective is to provide promising candidates, through a fast track and hands-on programme, with the necessary skills to take on their designated positions effectively. In all probability this will be an initiative specifically aimed at developing personnel to staff businesses established or acquired through mechanisms such as ownership trusts. In this context, people could be trained in participating companies and then released to take up designated positions in newly acquired organisations.

Development of the community: In a large number of instances, organisations have established relationships with communities with which they are in contact. The infrastructures of such communities is often either non-existent or poorly developed. Training of incumbents, particularly in administrative and financial skills, can be a major contribution in improving the level of skills within community organisations.

Participation in decision making: Participation in decision making is an important component of the challenge of broadening the management base. The largest part of the economically active population will not necessarily have direct economic ownership, but will rather be part of in-company participatory processes. Only when employees, irrespective of occupational level, experience the benefit of participation in company processes, can ownership of such processes be expected and its impact on productivity become a reality.

Effective participation is only possible once there is an ability to participate. This renders skills training in participatory processes such as decision making, problem solving, objective setting and action planning an essential part of any participatory process.

Addressing the business culture: An important question to be asked is whether business wants black faces or black skills. If skills are needed, then part of their development involves creation of a culture in the organisation that will accept a greater diversity of backgrounds, ideals and life styles.

Conclusion

Many companies are already exploring ways of meeting the challenge of broadening the ownership base. Unfortunately, very little is known of the work and efforts of business in this area. Consideration must be given to ways of ensuring that note is taken of the efforts by business and that acknowledgement is given when due.

In general, the challenge to build a real stake in the economy amongst the black community is an urgent social and economic imperative for business.

3

> ## Executive summary

Effective and legitimate business practices in the transition

This chapter focuses on a framework for business practices during the transition and suggests how these can be effected. Case studies of some companies which have successfully embarked upon such changes are included.

In addition to the primary role of business – creating wealth for the benefit of all its stakeholders – business also has a social role in the distribution of wealth. These two roles are dependent upon one another. As the state of the economy places the survival of business at stake, the motivation for business to change is primarily one of enlightened self-interest.

One could call this process 'in-house change'. The concept used here, though, is that of effective and legitimate business practices – 'effective' because only that will ensure that business performs its primary role; and 'legitimate' because without the acceptance of all stakeholders, and the moral legitimacy that brings, business will not be able to function optimally.

Obstacles as well as facilitating factors to changing existing business practices and establish effective and legitimate practices are pointed out in this chapter. In this regard, concepts such as normalisation and democratisation are important barometers of the kind of changes necessary.

Emphasis is placed squarely on establishing holistic (all-embracing), integrated and interdependent processes. Ten specific areas are pointed out:

☐ creating awareness of the need for change;
☐ aligning company strategy with the process of change;
☐ the establishment of unifying values;
☐ training and development;
☐ restructuring the decision making process;
☐ creating more satisfied customers;
☐ productivity, quality and pay-back;
☐ community involvement in development;
☐ labour relations;
☐ acknowledging the implications of fundamental change.

It is argued that if these ten areas can be systematically and holistically covered, business will have gone a long way in changing present business practices and established effective and legitimate processes conducive to the transition and continued growth into the 21st century.

In a section on practical guidelines, it is recommended that the starting point is to acknowledge that the various components of the change process are interdependent, and to plan on this basis. It is important to start with senior management and create an awareness of the need for establishing such practices, begin to align company strategy with this and acknowledge the implications of fundamental change for the organisation. Once this is established, it could be followed up by value sharing workshops as a starting point for participative processes. This should, importantly, be followed by the creation of what can be called a 'supportive climate' for participation by all employees in these processes. First change attitudes by means of value sharing workshops, and follow that by starting to change behaviour and the structures through which personnel interact and work together. There is, however, no quick fix to this time consuming process.

This section closes with five case studies from different companies which have made progress in some of the fields discussed.

Chapter Three

Effective and legitimate business practices in the transition

Many business leaders recognise that the transition they face demands the re-examination of present in-company business practices. This realisation has led to initiatives in areas such as equalising opportunity, technical skills training, participative management, social investment programmes, sensitisation programmes, life skills development, labour relations and affirmative action programmes, to name but a few.

The management of change associated with the transition in South Africa is especially relevant, given the major political, economic and social imbalances which exist. All of these have contributed to lack-lustre economic performance and dismal productivity.

The urgency of developing and refining an acceptable – and therefore legitimate – set of business practices is underscored by the immediacy of political transformation. A new government will be looking at business practices closely and considering whether legislative change is required in this area. Business may also find its internal practices measured against a bill of rights in a new constitution.

Changes in business practice will have to answer the question of 'what is in it for me?', likely to be posed by both management and the workforce. Benefits from the system must manifest themselves in reality, and participants need to experience such benefits directly. Trust will be developed, and commitment secured, only through delivery of benefits and experience.

To achieve a sound basis of trust and commitment, sincere processes of empowerment – through establishing the necessary structures for participation, capacity building, skill and capability enhancement and effective delivery of benefits – are essential. This applies both to in-company programmes and initiatives on a national basis.

It was against this background that CBM embarked on a process to provide its members with guidelines on 'in-house change', and ideas about the most effective manner to respond to the rapidly changing external environment. This chapter aims to provide a short history of and framework for the kind of business practices that are both conducive to the transition period, and allow for the effective management of change. This is an alternative to those changes being forced upon business, and endeavours to combine effectiveness with legitimacy.

A framework for business practice in transition

Business organisations need 'champions' to initiate and drive change. What follows are a set of guidelines that can be used by these 'champions' as a framework for effective and legitimate business practices.

The primary role of business

The primary role of business is to create wealth for the benefit of all its stakeholders. Without creating wealth, business cannot exist or survive. Wealth creation obviously includes job creation. Stakeholders include leaders, shareholders, management, employees and their representative bodies, customers and suppliers – in fact, the whole of society.

The pervasive perception and reality is that profit optimisation and shareholder paramouncy are still the primary driving forces behind business. This is not necessarily in keeping with the 'stakeholder' approach set out above.

Wealth creation is a long term process requiring immediate and urgent attention. If the old style of 'profit optimisation at all costs' is followed in the present situation, it will invariably lead to, amongst other things, retrenchments and negative growth. These are not in the long term interests of either the country or the individual company. A change of focus from the purely bottom-line profit-driven approach to a paradigm of wealth creation is necessary.

The social role of business

The social role of business is the distribution of created wealth. Business cannot survive without fulfilling this responsibility. This includes both the generation of wealth through economic growth and the development of society by addressing socio-economic needs.

These two roles of business are interdependent. If business does not create wealth it will not survive. If business does not play a responsible role with regard to the broader range of stakeholders – including the community – it will not survive.

All stakeholders need to examine how business can survive and prosper in the context of a deteriorating economy. Co-operation in dealing with the needs of all, rather than the destructive 'winner takes all' approach, needs to be examined. This principle should also apply during periods of economic strength.

The most important issues for business involve the need to survive in South Africa's changing society and the need for wealth creation. To this end, business must pursue labour stability and continuous improvement in performance and productivity. The strongest motivation for changing existing business practices during the transition is therefore self-interest. Business may be less capable of surviving and growing if it does not acknowledge this need.

Furthermore, with the democratisation of political life in South Africa, it is important that all South Africans share in the benefits of economic growth. The redistribution of power and knowledge, including information and expertise, is in the long term interests of the business community in that it is consistent with the 'stakeholder and wealth creation' approach.

Obstacles to effective and legitimate business practices

Certain important obstacles to changing existing business practices and establishing effective and legitimate practices can be noted:

☐ *organisational structures:* hierarchical structures, which emphasise (unilateral) 'managerial prerogative' tend to stifle creativity and productivity and block participation;

☐ *management style:* under an autocratic style of management people will, at best, work for mere survival rather than act creatively;

☐ *values and attitudes:* often rooted in racial or sexual prejudice, misperceptions and mistrust, these can seriously inhibit the development of common goals and motivation. Maintaining or merely reforming the status quo from the era of apartheid will obstruct the change process;

☐ *fears and aspirations:* the fears and insecurities of middle management (both black and white), as well as insufficient support for and communication with middle management about the overall direction of the company, can seriously impede progress. The aspirations and frustrations of workers – both black and white – are acknowledged obstacles;

☐ *lack of communication and information:* a culture of top-down management and secrecy results in poor or no communication and lack of information. This is not conducive to employees taking responsibility for the company;

☐ *lack of education and training:* due to the poor education system, businesses have an inability to grow from within their own ranks. Illiteracy and a skills shortage in the job market make matters worse. An external obstacle in this regard is the way in which business schools focus on administrative managerial training, instead of additionally providing practical training.

These and other obstacles will have to be addressed in the new South Africa. Within each company, an environment will have to be created which will be conducive to the normalisation of attitudes and relationships. This will, of necessity, precede an improvement in performance and productivity.

Facilitating effective and legitimate business practices

In much the same way, important facilitating factors can be listed:

☐ *a participative environment:* the innovative and creative capacity of people will be developed and enhanced if they are directly involved in decisions affecting their lives. This means, inter alia, that systems of shared responsibility and leadership should be created within business;

☐ *the creation of trust and security:* people perform well within a climate of trust where fears, prejudices and misconceptions can be dealt with openly. Lifelong employment provides employees with security and trust in each other, and in the company. If middle management can be assured of job security, it is less likely to feel threatened by change and could even help to facilitate it;

☐ *a shared value system:* such a climate can only be created if a shared value system is mutually developed and practically implemented. It is important that business organisations go through the process of identifying, developing and implementing shared values: this in itself is a learning process for both management and employees. These values include common goals for the business and for the country, acceptance of each other's human dignity, and sharing responsibility for the company's future;

☐ a *'pioneer of change'* : this is an obvious and crucial facilitator of change in a company. It is increasingly accepted that this change agent must be the chief executive or someone working directly under his/her guidance. This person should be empowered and equipped to direct the process of change within the company.

Normalisation and democratisation

As in the political arena, both the normalisation and the democratisation of business is essential.

Normalisation involves rectification of past injustices, including the elimination of race and sex discrimination in the workplace, the acceptance of justice and dignity for all, the creation of equal opportunities and the changing of attitudes. In all of this, it is important not to fall into the trap of tokenism, but equally important not to use anti-tokenism as an excuse to avoid addressing inequalities.

Democratisation involves the pro-active creation of a dynamic culture for business, the environment in which it operates and, ultimately, the future. The democratisation of the workplace could include some of the issues referred to above, as well as the following possible initiatives:

☐ open disclosure of information;
☐ the creation of an 'intelligent' and learning organisation in which each participant has a meaningful role and optimum responsibility;
☐ the continuous improvement of each employee;
☐ the creation of equal opportunities, by means of affirmative action and accelerated training;
☐ the creation of more jobs;
☐ a commitment to address critical community issues such as education, violence and housing, through involvement in community development.

The process of democratisation, at the same time, could incorporate controversial approaches such as worker control, co-determination and representation on boards. These matters need to be confronted head-on rather than being avoided. If left unresolved, these issues can, and do, impact negatively on the workplace and business environment.

Establishing effective and legitimate business practices is an integrated and interdependent process

Changing existing business practices should not be initiated or handled in an ad hoc way, and should be approached as part of an holistic and integrated process. It is, for example, not enough to address only the 'sensitisation' of the workforce without addressing its training and development needs. It is impossible, especially because of external political and socio-economic factors, to view the workplace or any aspect of it in isolation. Fragmented processes can result in even more problems than experienced before.

It is equally important to identify and agree on the respective roles of the different participants or stakeholders, and accept that the process is an interdependent one. For example, the commitment of organised labour to help change present business practices may be directly related to the degree to which those initiatives are perceived to undermine the role of the unions. Common ground between different stakeholders such as labour and management should, therefore, be sought so that shared commitment can be developed. Without a commitment to interdependence by all participants, any initiative is doomed to failure.

Finally, it is important to realise that the establishment of effective and legitimate business practices is a process that can only be achieved through concerted medium-to-long term strategy and effort.

Ten key areas in establishing effective and legitimate business practices

Ten key areas have the potential to form the parameters of effective and legitimate business practices. It is important to note, however, that open, honest communication within business organisations is a prerequisite to the establishment of effective and legitimate business practices and should be seen as part and parcel of each of the key areas set out below:

☐ creating awareness of the need for changing existing business practices and establishing effective and legitimate ones;
☐ aligning company strategy with this process;
☐ establishing unifying values;
☐ training and development;

☐ restructuring the decision making process;
☐ creating more satisfied customers;
☐ productivity, quality and pay-back;
☐ community involvement in development;
☐ labour relations;
☐ acknowledging the implications of fundamental change.

The ten key areas and their challenge to business

In an earlier phase focusing on 'in-house change', the CBM conducted workshops and a question and answer survey of its member companies. The ten key areas were described in 'statements of objective' and senior management was requested to evaluate each area in terms of its currently perceived 'status' (what is seen as being done at present) and 'desirability' (what should be done in future). This formed the basis for a quantitative and qualitative analysis, and for change management specialists to evaluate the results.

The full findings of this research are available from the CBM Head Office. However, in summary, the following emerged:

☐ a very real awareness of the need for changing present practices and establishing effective and legitimate business practices exists in the ranks of senior management;
☐ business has moved out of its earlier stages of resistance to change, and is trying to bridge the gap between desirability and status. There may, however, be some organisations where not only inability to implement change, but even unwillingness, exists;
☐ there is a significant difference in perceptions between members of management who have not been exposed to a detailed micro- and macro-scenario covering South Africa's economic, social and political status and conditions, and those who have. There is a tendency to complacency amongst those who have not been so exposed;
☐ although there is a generally high level of good intention regarding change, this is not backed up with sufficient understanding of the dynamics, commitment and allocation of resources. Change objectives are, in all probability, not being included effectively in organisational monitoring, recognition and reward systems;
☐ there is a very real danger that business could become increasingly out of kilter with broader macro-changes. If business chooses to remain relatively intransigent by comparison with macro-socio-political

changes, there is a real possibility that political power will be used to enforce change in business.

The ten key areas and specific challenges

Creating awareness of the need for changing present practices

Although change is a natural phenomenon in life, it does not happen automatically or naturally. In South African society the alienation wrought by apartheid has created deeply rooted social memories (including stereotyped perceptions) which inhibit constructive interpersonal relationships. This historic alienation between races and consequent misperceptions requires that change be 'driven'. A prerequisite for this is the creation of awareness of the need for change. This has to be undertaken with employees and management participating on an equal basis. Successful businesses in the new South Africa need to address these issues before being able to achieve their full economic potential.

This area recorded a fairly low status in the research. Two factors contributed to this: management underestimates the need to address the creation of this awareness because it has accepted change as inevitable; and management feels that there are more pressing and 'tangible' priorities, such as productivity improvements. Either way, it is a fallacy to imagine that this basic step can be 'skipped'. Mistrust and misperception will inhibit, if not destroy, any positive effects other measures might have. Indeed, mutual trust and constructive personal relationships are prerequisites for changing present practices and establishing effective and legitimate business practices in the transition and thereafter.

Challenges in this regard include the following:

☐ perceptions of management and employees, both black and white, have to be addressed as a prerequisite for creating relationships based on mutual trust and respect. If this matter is not addressed, then all other endeavours will remain hamstrung by past perceptions, mistrust and apprehensions;

☐ this can best be done through facilitated and structured workshops addressing perceptions, fears, prejudices and hopes openly and honestly, within the context of a macro-scenario of the 'new' South Africa;

☐ another possibility is to expose both employees and management to macro-scenarios for the future political economy.

*Aligning company strategy with the process of
changing present business practices*

If a company's primary objective, namely to remain in business, is not
fulfilled then all other issues become hypothetical. In order to optimise the
achievement of this goal in South Africa, management needs to dedicate
itself continuously to promoting full recognition of each individual, justice, equality of opportunity and the creation of wealth.

If creating awareness of the need for establishing effective and
legitimate business practices is a first step, the next is to ensure that this is
not a 'once-off' initiative and that the company's medium and long term
strategy is aligned with this need. This makes good business sense and
should be linked to processes that will align not only the company strategy
to change, but also align the entire workforce to these strategies. This
necessitates a system of participation by all employees and management.
Furthermore, it is important that senior management accepts that change
is an essential part of staying in business and that the company's medium
and long term strategy is aligned with this.

The research findings conclude that little or no progress has been
made in this regard. Although difficult to determine, the primary reasons
for this could be the fear of management of 'losing control', an autocratic
management style and a lack of trust in employees to act responsibly and
in the interests of the business.

The challenges that businesses face in this regard include:

☐ convincing senior management that it is a prerequisite to align the
company's strategy with the goal of changing present practices;
☐ discussing, at a senior management level, concepts usually seen as
'dangerous' (eg information sharing) in a structured way to demytholo-
gise them and open up creative possibilities. In preparing senior
management for this, it is essential that they are exposed to the micro-
and macro-socio-political issues of the day;
☐ preparing and empowering chief executive officers to play the role of
'champions of change'.

The establishment of unifying and shared values

Within the diversity of cultures, races and political opinions, it is important
to establish commonalities within a business. Given South Africa's unfor-
tunate past and the diverse views of employees regarding the nature and
purpose of the business, it is essential for all employees to be called upon
to focus on and develop a common set of values. This cannot be done

through a 'top-down' process, but should be undertaken in a participative and 'bottom-up' process. Structured workshops of different stakeholders and levels are necessary to achieve this. The process of establishing common values creates a shared commitment and loyalty to the business by all stakeholders and provides impetus for the establishment of effective and legitimate business practices. 'Values' in this context refer to concepts such as:

☐ a democratic culture;
☐ non-racism and non-sexism;
☐ participation and shared responsibility;
☐ open and honest communication;
☐ equal opportunity and justice in the workplace;
☐ recognition of the dignity and equality of every employee.

A high level of difference between 'status' and 'desirability' was recorded in the research. This difference indicates that, although a willingness exists to explore this area, no concerted action has been taken. In some instances, vision and values for businesses have been determined by senior management unilaterally. These cannot be called common values, nor can they create the shared commitment referred to above. Several guidelines can be identified in this regard:

☐ the establishment of shared values is pivotal to the changing of present practices and the establishment of effective and legitimate business practices, as it lays the foundation of a commonly shared goal for the business;
☐ these values cannot be established by management in a top-down process, but need to be developed through a consultative process involving all levels of the business;
☐ facilitated workshops again are a way of achieving this;
☐ even after the joint establishment of these values, it is important to ensure that all stakeholders are able to change their attitudes and behaviour accordingly. Structures have to be created in businesses to facilitate this change;
☐ even though seemingly laborious, these processes have the advantage of strengthening the awareness of the need for change and highlighting the interdependence and mutually beneficial roles of all stakeholders.

Training and development

The development of human capital is internationally accepted as a prerequisite for performance and growth. Against the background of an acute skills shortage, lack of managers and the education crisis, this requires particular attention in overcoming the inequalities created by apartheid. It is therefore of the utmost importance that training and development within businesses become a priority. This is the only way for South African companies to improve productivity, quality and competitiveness. This, in turn, can only be achieved if people are viewed as a long term investment – as human capital, and not a mere cost factor.

The research findings clearly showed that the need for training and development is widely acknowledged. But it is also clear that little or no progress has been made in this regard. Training and development in companies is largely still planned or conducted with little or no input from those who are subjected to such programmes.

Challenges arising from this area include the following:

☐ as with shared values, training and development needs and strategies cannot be established unilaterally. Employees and trade unions should be part of the process of determining these needs and strategies;
☐ relevant issues in this regard include literacy programmes, opportunities for career development and courses assisting employees to understand how the business works;
☐ the possibility of a 'ban' on recruiting employees at certain levels from outside the company could be considered. This would indicate that management is serious about training and development and views employees as investments and assets;
☐ another option is for a negotiated and mutually audited percentage of the business' profits to be allocated to the training and development of employees;
☐ if training and development is managed in a participative way, it can have extremely beneficial effects, not only for strengthening the process of change within the business, but also for improving productivity and quality.

Restructuring the decision making process

This key area is one of the most difficult to understand and address because of misperceptions associated with it. Without oversimplifying the matter, it means that employees participate in making decisions that affect their working lives directly. This process should take place on different levels, and could develop maturity and co-responsibility in employees. International and some significant local experience have demonstrated that continuous improvement of wealth creation is greatly enhanced by involving all employees in the process of decision making about issues that affect them. Not only does this promote personal identification with the company's objectives, but it enhances motivation and commitment to the business as a whole – even if final decisions are contrary to the individual's recommendations or preferences.

From the responses obtained in the research referred to above, it is clear that this key area has the greatest discrepancy between status and desirability. Several challenges can be easily identified in this regard:

☐ clarification of what is meant by the concept, perhaps in the workshops for senior management mentioned above. Relevant issues to be raised include access to information about the business; participation by employees in the recruitment and promotion of supervisors/managers and their evaluation; participation by employee representatives in strategic planning processes; and co-responsibility by management and employees for the overall values, goals and objectives of the business;

☐ addressing management fears that democratisation means that trade unions/employees are going to 'take over', that they will not be able to carry the responsibilities because of poor training or education or that they will abuse their decision making power;

☐ it is not possible to achieve a performance-driven organisation in which employees feel that they have a 'stake' in the business if hierarchical management styles persist. It is therefore necessary to consider ways and means of creating co-responsibility between workers and management on issues that affect the work and lives of those workers directly, including productivity;

☐ it is not possible to restructure the decision making process successfully without first having fulfilled the objectives of three other key areas: creating awareness of the need for change, establishing shared values, and acknowledging the implications of fundamental change. Experience has proven that this is especially true where relations at the interface between primarily white supervisors and primarily black employees have not been addressed.

Creating more satisfied customers

The ultimate objective of any company is continuously to create more customers in ways that ensure satisfaction with the company's services and products. This requires integrating the entire process from primary producer of raw materials through to the final consumer. It necessitates the creation of what can be called an 'open pipeline' through which value is added to the product at every phase. It also requires a focus on the satisfaction of the 'internal customer's' needs within the business as well as those of the external customer.

The creation of more customers as a key area is closely linked to wealth creation, productivity and unemployment. It should be seen as more than 'service with a smile' but as one of the areas requiring strategic planning and dedication.

The research findings indicate that, although appreciated as making good business sense, the concept of interdependent 'pipelining' or 'value-adding' is not yet sufficiently understood, nor is there a commitment to this in the context of creating more satisfied customers.

The challenges posed in this area are clear:

☐ the concept of interdependent pipelining and its possible benefits should be discussed and promoted strongly within and between companies. This should again be done in a facilitated and structured way: both within the business involving all stakeholders and internal and external consumers, and on a sectoral basis between competitors;
☐ by doing this, the often adversarial or independent relationships leading to 'bottlenecks' in the 'pipelines' can be transformed into interdependent relations and partnerships in wealth and customer creation.

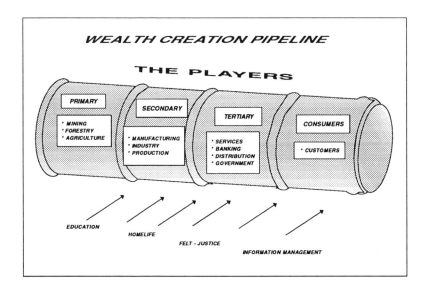

Productivity, quality and 'pay-back'

'Pay-back' is a term used for the fruits of higher productivity and better quality that should 'come back' to the employee in the form of, for example, higher wages or bonuses.

This area represents a real challenge to South African businesses, given the poor record of productivity improvement in the country. Productivity and quality are integral to the process of wealth creation. While some productivity gains can be achieved by improved mechanisation, this process is greatly enhanced by encouraging employees to participate in goal setting and providing just rewards for their incremental successes ('pay-back'). Productivity, quality and pay-back are acid tests for effective in-house change. If change does not ultimately lead to improvement in these areas, it is not worth embarking upon. There is, furthermore, a close relationship between these areas, the external environment affecting the business and other in-house change endeavours. It is an area where the 'effectiveness' of business practices has to meet the 'legitimacy' of those same practices.

Linkages between productivity and quality improvements and the following factors are not disputed by the research findings:

☐ enhanced employee skills and competence, and a stable home environment;
☐ employee participation, both in setting goals and in the establishment of the reward system to promote the attainment of these goals;
☐ employee understanding of how direct performance impacts on overall company performance and how, in turn, this benefits the individual employee;
☐ employee confidence that productivity gains will not lead to short term retrenchment.

The emerging challenges in this area are the following:

☐ business organisations should take the interdependence between productivity and quality improvements, a stable home environment and enhanced employee skills seriously. Education, stable home and family life, the capacity to use information and perceived justice should therefore be addressed urgently by companies;
☐ improvements in productivity should not be used to create short term redundancies. If this happens in the long term, employees should be

given sufficient time and training to develop alternative careers or to find alternative jobs;
☐ productivity and quality improvement should be seen as some of the end results of a long process. There is no 'quick' solution to the problem;
☐ the emphasis should be on total employee involvement in order to produce sustained productivity gains, rather than short term and volatile gains resulting from top-down autocratic or paternalistic management styles;
☐ employees should perceive and experience that it is to their benefit to improve productivity and quality through being fairly rewarded for their efforts.

Involvement in community development ('social responsibility')

The circumstances of the community within which a business operates are both affected by that business and impacts on it in turn. It is both beneficial to, and a responsibility of, a business to become involved in the development of that community because of the interdependence of productivity and external circumstances.

Participative processes employed within business should be extended into the field of community development. The needs of the community and processes to address those needs can only be established in consultation and co-determination with the community itself. Old-style paternalism and charity hand-outs no longer suffice. This also applies to what is called 'social responsibility'.

There are indications that there has been little effective company involvement in community development as a participative process.

This challenges business in the following ways:

☐ on the basis of an integrated approach to business practice, companies should not view 'social responsibility' as 'a nice thing to do' or charity hand-out, but as a social investment in the future of the company;
☐ the establishment of the development needs of communities should be co-determined by the communities, relevant trade unions, development agencies and business;
☐ companies should not only provide financial assistance to communities, but also make their expertise, infrastructure and time available to ensure, as joint partners, that funds are optimally used. This includes ensuring that unacceptable quantities of funds are not used to administer the self-same funds. Business organisations should therefore become actively involved in community development at a regional and local level;

☐ the aim of involvement in community development should be to create self-management and ownership by communities and thereby strengthen community structures.

Labour relations

The recognition agreements of the 1980s, and their impact upon organisational development and power relationships in the workplace, laid the foundation for an exceptionally rapid development in trade union-management relationships. The interdependence of the different key areas and the emphasis on a participative culture make it clear that constructive relations between management and trade unions are of the utmost importance for effective change in business practices. Without joint commitment and even company-level 'social contracts' between management and trade unions, effective change and consequent increases in productivity and wealth creation cannot occur. Where change in business practices has occurred in companies without the participation of trade unions, it has often been opposed by them. Given the state of the economy and the interdependence of management and labour, options for co-determination should be continuously investigated as a matter of urgency.

Notwithstanding a high desirability rating, the status of this area in the research findings is fairly low, given its obvious importance. This may be explained by the adversarial and politicised nature of labour relations during the past decade. There is, nevertheless, a willingness on the part of management to at least explore the possibilities of co-determination and partnerships with unions. A number of mutually agreed productivity-linked bonus schemes testify to this factor.

Given the present high political profile of the trade union movement and the fact that it wants to establish itself as an independent player in the political economy, this willingness could be tested quite strongly in the not too distant future. On the other hand, the positive and constructive role that trade unions are at present playing in the National Economic Forum counterbalances this perspective.

Several guidelines and challenges emerge in this area:

☐ businesses should use recognition agreements as the foundation on which to build sound relations with unions;
☐ it is necessary to explore and create systems and structures in which co-determination and partnerships (a win-win situation) are possible between management and unions;

☐ it is important to accept trade unions, not as a 'necessary evil', but as joint partners and essential contributors in the process of wealth creation. It is therefore important for management to empower trade unions through appointing full-time shop stewards, and through providing facilities and training. In engaging unions, management should demand reciprocity in this respect, so that unions also view business as an essential contributor to the joint wealth creation process;

☐ the usual adversarial relationship between management and the unions should be addressed as a matter of urgency, to move to one of consensus seeking and co-operation. This could be done by involving the unions from the beginning in the process of changing present practices. In this way, management could indicate that it respects the trade unions as an important stakeholder.

Acknowledging the implications of fundamental change

Although this might seem self-evident, it is important to stress that fundamental change does not happen easily and that it has serious implications for business. Change cannot be addressed half-heartedly or in an ad hoc-fashion, and demands the changing not only of attitudes, but also of structures and systems. This takes time and can be painful. It requires patience, endurance and wisdom and a medium term dedication to a driven process. It is a challenge that cannot, however, be rejected.

From the research findings, it is evident that, although management accepts that change has fundamental implications, there is confusion between intent and actual commitment to fundamental change within the business community. This key area is as fundamental to establishing effective and legitimate business practices as creating awareness and aligning company strategy with the process.

The challenges posed by this area include the following:

☐ the most important and fundamental point is that changing present business practices cannot be a 'quick-fix' of problems experienced by business. It is at least a medium term process requiring planning, drive and patience. It also needs joint strategic planning and monitoring;

☐ this process is costly, both in terms of finances and emotional strain;

☐ to ensure that the process has long term positive effects, it is necessary to approach it in an holistic and integrated way, as well as to create structures conducive to participative and interdependent processes;

☐ this should be accepted by management, and especially by the chief executive officer, without whom this process cannot start or be carried through. It should also be accepted by shareholders, in the company's and their own best interests.

Practical possibilities for establishing effective and legitimate business practices

☐ Follow an holistic and integrated approach to the ten key areas (and others). This is the key to ensuring a successful outcome. It is essential to avoid an ad hoc and disjointed approach. Planning must be holistic and strategic.

☐ Acknowledge and plan around the interdependence of the various components of effective and legitimate business practices.Consciously acknowledge and plan around the fact that the ten key areas (and others that might be identified in business) are interdependent.

☐ Start with senior management to create an awareness of the need for establishing effective and legitimate business practices. Align company strategy with this and acknowledge the implications of fundamental change.

☐ Senior management in general, and the chief executive officer specifically, are responsible for initiating and 'driving the establishment of effective and legitimate business practices. Senior management therefore has to be 'on board' before the planning and implementation process can begin.

☐ Making business practices legitimate should not be viewed as a 'nice to do' extra dealing with 'affirmative action', but a strategic decision to survive and grow into the 21st century. It should be planned and executed as part of company strategy and driven primarily by the line management and not purely human resource managers.

☐ It is important to create the capacity within the company to deal with this process. Consultants and specialists should be used to help set up in-house structures and empower human resources staff to establish and run effective and legitimate business practices themselves.

☐ Follow this up by value sharing workshops, using them as the starting point for participative processes. The establishment of common and unifying values should be seen as a key priority. In this way the other stakeholders, specifically employees and trade unions, are brought into the process from a very early stage. It is important not to start planning the process of establishing effective and legitimate business practices before common values and commitment have been established in a participative way. It is also important to address the issues of business culture and different cultures and values in the workshops.

☐ Create a 'supportive climate' for participation by all employees. Depending on the specific company's circumstances, creative structures should be formed through which employees and management can continue to interact and participate in a structured way. This probably demands that literacy and language barriers will have to be addressed through an intensive literacy programme. It also means that effort should be put into the creative and participative structures to let people (especially managers) listen and obtain get feedback. In this way, people will have opportunities to continue the implementation of the values that were commonly established.

☐ Such structures will create the opportunity for more creative and joint thinking with regard to the difficult issues of continuous improvement, 'affirmative action', enhancing of employees' business and economic understanding, and life skills and technical training.

In summary, first change attitudes by means of value sharing workshops. Thereafter, it is necessary (not optional) to start changing people's behaviour and the structures in which they interact and work together. When these structures are in place and working, other priorities can start to be addressed in a meaningful way. Throughout this process, the importance of effective and honest communication cannot be overemphasised. The building of trust is crucial, and will be seen in information disclosure, participation and jointly agreed codes of conduct. It is also crucial, during this process, for companies to evaluate the effectiveness of the strategies on a continuous basis. In any transition, the environment can change quickly, making a revision and change of strategy necessary.

Conclusion

Change in present business practices and the establishment of legitimate business practices are not 'quick fixes' to the problems of business. The processes described above will take 18 to 24 months at the very least. Other, even more difficult, key areas such as productivity can only be addressed successfully after this, and may even take longer. In companies where this approach has been followed, it has proved to be an effective process with which to address these complex issues. The ultimate challenge is to combine democracy with profitability, and demonstrate this in practise.

Case studies

Nampak

It is generally accepted within the Nampak Group, comprising some 19 different businesses, over 120 factories and 22 000 people, that continued growth, retention of its competitiveness and, in some cases, survival of particular businesses, cannot be ensured purely through capital investment and/or professional management.

It follows that a major investment in what has been termed 'people driven growth' is necessary for the continued prosperity of the group, its employees, shareholders, suppliers and customers.

There are four pillars that underpin the people driven growth strategy in Nampak, viz social investment, black advancement, training and development and the in-house change process. It is the integration of these four pillars and the numerous initiatives that emerge out of them that gives the group the confidence that the work undertaken in the area will provide group businesses with strategic commercial advantages.

The in-house change process

One of the key pillars to this people driven growth strategy is the commencement of an in-house change process. This process began in 1991 at a strategy workshop involving the top hierarchy of management within the group. Here it was accepted that major transformation processes were needed to ensure that the majority of people employed in the group had a common sense of purpose, focus and vision, shared a common set of values and were committed to making the group, in the words of the chairman and the managing director of Nampak, a 'world beater'.

In simple terms, the process entails the following steps:

☐ an awareness phase which involves a number of workshops with management, shop stewards and informal leadership, to create the awareness and energy to commence the in-house change process (significant lobbying and discussion takes place at this point);
☐ commencement of a vision and value sharing process with the leadership in the company (worker and management), followed by value sharing workshops throughout the operations ensuring that every single

employee participates in the process of developing a shared vision and common values;
☐ what emerges from this particular process is a new structural arrangement in the form of a steering committee driving a number of different changes and initiatives in the operation. These include the monitoring of 'living the shared values identified', developing the new participative structures for the effective management of the operation, and setting up structures for the management of vital areas such as literacy training, skills training and productivity/quality enhancement;
☐ the next phase involves the setting up of these structures and creating the capacity for ensuring that they deliver not only in terms of the operation's performance but actually empower employees to become part of the whole process of creating wealth and participation in the value added chain through to ultimate customer satisfaction;
☐ the last phase involves continuous improvement and the development of appropriate reward structures linked to the increased wealth generated by the whole process.

The process itself is painful, as it involves undoing locked-in prejudices, structures, the 'baggage' of apartheid, etc, but already in the early stages of the in-house change process one has seen the enormous enthusiasm and commitment to common goals by people involved in the process. One has seen the reduction of absenteeism, increased productivity and quality, stabilisation of industrial relations and the creation of participative structures, etc. An example of such a structure is the development in one of the operations of 'cells' – multi-skilled task teams which manage and control the production process from raw material to delivery.

Essential criteria for the success of the in-house change process have been developed as a result of hard won experience. Some of these are:

☐ the whole process should be linked and integrated with an overall people driven growth strategy. An example of this is that in social investment initiatives, the criteria developed for any initiative states that it must have passed a consultation test and must benefit employees or their dependents. One such initiative, which links in very firmly with the in-house change process, allows the children of employees to attend previously whites only technical colleges to attain a 'technical matric'. The selection is undertaken by committees consisting of educationalists, community/civic representatives and shop stewards;

- □ 'change agents' with solid records in the so-called 'struggle' could be appointed. These individuals are key in the whole awareness/lobbying phase of the in-house change process;
- □ use of consultants who have experience in the democratisation of workplaces;
- □ obtaining sincere commitment and drive from the most senior level of the group;
- □ use of the consultation process on an on-going basis (this cannot be underestimated). For the process to be successful, one has continually to consult management, foremen, shop stewards, trade union officials, community representatives and other stakeholders;
- □ the whole process must be driven by a commercial rationale. There is no altruism involved in the in-house change process, and its foundation is built on the survival, growth and competitiveness of various businesses;
- □ the nature of the process is a democratic one, in the sense that it is born of discussion, debate and negotiation at the lowest level and is not an imposed process. This is often the reason for failure of total quality/ participation initiatives which have a top-down approach. Workers need to identify with participative structures that they have had a hand in developing, linked to a shared vision and set of common values, again which they have had a hand in developing;
- □ a major pillar of the whole people driven growth strategy is training and development and one cannot underestimate the amount of time, effort and money that has to be dedicated to this process to enhance not only the in-house change process, but also the development of participative structures, black advancement and social investment;
- □ the process confronts the traditional hierarchical structures and historic process of management control and it should be noted that this ingrained system is one which is exceptionally difficult to change. On-going commitment for the whole process is therefore vital if such hurdles are to be overcome.

The PG Bison National Forum

Towards joint responsibility for growth

PG Bison's National Forum is an attempt to introduce principles of negotiation – not just consultation – into the formulation of corporate policies and practices affecting the lives of the workforce.

In 1987, PG Bison launched a change process called 'Total Productivity and Quality' (TPQ). This focused on changing the group's culture and values to prepare for a post-apartheid South Africa, in the belief that personal growth and improved productivity would follow.

PG Bison manufactures board products and durable surfaces such as formica at its Bisonboard and Laminate Industries plants, and distributes them through a network of PG Wood outlets. The group employs more that 4 000 people and has recognition agreements with four different unions.

Initial TPQ steps included value-sharing sessions in which blacks and whites met for two full days of discussions to explore their fears and hopes for the future. Managers visited employees' homes and hostels and went to Zimbabwe to meet executives of the ANC before it was legalised.

At factory level, participative processes began to be introduced, built around natural work teams known in-house as 'In-A-Groups'. A growing team of full-time change agents created these participative systems, as well as basic adult education programmes, including literacy.

The unions, however, worried that the programme was being imposed on them. In 1989, shop stewards formed an elected national shop stewards committee, unusual in its cross-union makeup and its inclusion of an Uwusa contingent. In 1990, the committee, including union officials, declared the suspension of TPQ on the grounds that it had not been negotiated with the unionised workforce. The entire initiative appeared in jeopardy.

The National Forum

After months of debate, a joint management-worker meeting was held in March 1991, with union organisers among the 40 delegates. At this meeting, the company directly acknowledged the right of the unionised workforce to negotiate, not just consult, and the worker caucus accepted the resumption of the TPQ process.

The two sides agreed to form the PG Bison National Forum to negotiate issues of common concern. The agenda for the first forum ranged from information sharing to values to centralised bargaining and full-time shop stewards. A joint organising committee was formed to prepare the first National Forum, scheduled for June 1991. That forum, held at the Dikhololo Conference Centre near Brits, brought together 60 delegates from PG Bison operations for two days of intense debate. By the closing session, the two sides had negotiated a series of accords:

☐ agreement on the role and purpose of the forum as a representative body consisting of managerial and worker representatives with the mandate to negotiate and formulate broad company principles, philosophy, policies and values for the business. Decisions taken will be referred to Strategic Business Unit (SBU) Leadership Teams for implementation. The forum does not replace existing collective bargaining processes, nor affect rights covering strike actions or lockouts;
☐ the forum is a problem solving body requiring the sharing of information and thorough debate. The prevailing values should be 'freedom of association and opinion'. Agreement on membership specified two shop stewards from each of the eight SBUs, two management delegates per site, five head office managers and five trade union officials – a total of 42 delegates (with support staff to attend as well);
☐ approval of guidelines for the group's education programme, called LEAP (Learning for Empowerment and Progress), including a stipulation that new programmes be negotiated with the shop stewards and that Cosatu be consulted;
☐ agreement on the regular disclosure of company performance information to the workforce at both group and SBU level;
☐ agreement on participative structures, from In-A-Groups at departmental level to SBU Leadership Teams and the National Forum itself;
☐ agreement to negotiate the demand for centralised bargaining on wages and working conditions at divisional level (Bisonboard and PG Wood had traditionally bargained at site level);
☐ agreement on a policy for full-time paid shop stewards.

Several other areas were either too complex or too new to resolve in the first meeting. Joint worker-manager task forces were appointed to investigate the issues of human resource development, community involvement, health and safety, employee housing and the issue of representation for non-unionised workers in the forum.

At the second forum held in October at the Hunter's Rest conference centre, the process moved forward – while deadlocking on the thorny question of whether and how to include non-unionised employees, who make up nearly one-third of PG Bison's workforce. The second forum committed the group to 100 per cent literacy of the workforce within five years; created a mechanism for reportbacks from SBUs on progress in implementing agreements as a method of monitoring compliance; and approved the statement of values and objectives, which had been circulated in draft form for debate.

The third forum in March 1992 approved a task force proposal on broadening employee housing assistance, while the issue of non-unionised employee membership in the forum was shelved temporarily. Reportbacks on progress at the factories raised questions, however, on whether the forum's agreements were actually being carried out.

Union delegates, who two years earlier had demanded the suspension of TPQ, called on management to work together to find ways to deepen and accelerate the change process and its participative programmes. The unions proposed that the forum organising committee be transformed into a monitoring body which would measure implementation and provide operational support for the change initiatives.

That proposal represented a new phase in the evolution of the forum; the unionised workers had taken the initiative in pushing PG Bison toward full implementation of the group's Total Productivity and Quality philosophy. As Elijah Mansinga, a Ppwawu organiser, said at the second national forum:

What we have done here is not small. It is very big. We are makers of history, of the new South Africa. This is not easy, there are no set rules, no precedent to follow. We are pioneers of the new industrial order of South Africa.

Premier Group awareness programme

'Premier in the new South Africa'

The dramatic announcements made by the State President on 2 February 1990 and the unbanning of political organisations which followed, prompted senior Premier management to question whether Premier and its people were ready to enter the new South Africa. Its chairman, Peter Wrighton, felt that the company should be pro-active and develop a vehicle which could provide an opportunity for people further down the line to give their views on the political changes taking place, and the idea of an awareness programme was born.

Phase one of the 'Awareness Programme' consisted of a video entitled 'Premier in the new South Africa' which carried the views of senior management on the changes taking place. The plan was to show the material widely in the organisation in workshops, and to provide a forum for debate and individual input. The theme of the project was how Premier should adapt to the political changes taking place to become a winning corporation in the future.

Some 80 people were trained as facilitators to handle discussions flowing from the video. In addition, a number of one day workshops were also held, focusing on political changes and providing employees with information and understanding.

Employees were asked to identify the most important environmental, market and employee pressures facing the company, and to discuss how the company could grow under these circumstances. The workshops identified six broad answers to this question:

☐ communication inside the group needed to be improved;
☐ interactive management should be promoted and developed;
☐ informal and formal discrimination must be eradicated;
☐ education training and development plans should be identified;
☐ corporate social investment should be developed;
☐ the mission statement must be put into practice.

Phase one of the programme met with varying degrees of involvement. In some cases, line management was reluctant to take the process down to shop floor level. In some plants the majority union objected as it felt that its members were not involved in the planning of the project. However, in some plants the video was shown to groups of employees at all levels in the organisation, and the reaction was very positive.

It was decided to embark on phase two of the awareness programme, by inviting senior union leadership to assist with the planning process. A second video was developed which took the form of a panel debate involving senior management and union executives on Premier's place in the new South Africa.

The focus of the second video is on identifying the progress or lack thereof the company has made toward implementing its mission statement and resolving the issues identified in the first video. More broadly, employees are asked how the company can assist in the removal of obstacles to a political settlement in South Africa. The panel discussions have been videoed, and facilitators are in the process of being briefed. Response from the union has been positive, and it is anticipated that contact groups will meet down to the shop floor.

Some lessons can be learnt from the Premier experience:

☐ it is essential to include the union in the planning of any project of this nature. Without this involvement, workers will be suspicious of the company's motives and will not participate;
☐ competent facilitators should be identified and trained to handle the group discussions and to aid the process;
☐ line management should be kept informed and taken along with the process if it is to succeed.

In summary, the Awareness Programme has proved to be a valuable project which has helped to create better relationships across the company. Premier has found that the vast majority of employees are concerned with the future of the company in the new South Africa, and are keen on building better relationships on the shop floor, rather than engaging in conflictual processes.

Eskom quality programme, Durban

*The involvement of employees in the transition to a
new Eskom through participation in quality circles*

This change was initiated in 1985 and can perhaps best be illustrated by
the following process:

☐ Eskom restructures to meet the changing environment and unleashes a
company Mission, Strategy and Philosophy (MSP) to guide the change
process;
☐ this process is participatory and involves a massive retraining programme via workshops, team building and 'management walkabouts';
☐ decentralisation and delegation of authority are key aspects alongside
'customer focus, superior performance and mutual respect'. The team
concept is introduced via quality circles (QCs). The spirit is to support
delegation and decentralisation through participative problem solving;
☐ quality circle technology is adapted to the Natal/KwaZulu environment
and introduced as a voluntary employee involvement programme. Key
stated motives include employee development, improved customer
service, enhanced quality and productivity, better quality of work life
(*Izinga Lempilo*), and asking employees to help make Eskom contribute
to a better South Africa/Natal;
☐ widespread training (scenarios, problem solving, etc) occurs. Participation is widespread with some areas having 100 per cent participation.
(Total number of people involved in the programme, 1 000, which is
equal to 54 per cent of business unit);
☐ a unique problem solving process is developed by employees and
enhanced techniques/processes such as 'total lifecycle management' are
introduced to ensure that benefits from solutions can be obtained. This
includes the patents and joint venture agreements with manufacturers
to commercialise inventions;
☐ management and supervisory levels go through a steep learning curve
as employees start questioning and making decisions in terms of their
new authority. Company leadership learns that their role is now to
facilitate. Autocratic rule is no longer acceptable as part of the culture;
☐ a solution journal is developed to distribute solutions quickly in a
colourful, one page format, to all other teams, customers and suppliers.
This gives recognition to the teams but also helps to spread the benefit
of the solution;

☐ trade unions, through shop stewards, are also actively involved in QCs from the beginning as they see the merit of the quality of life approach adopted. Their authority or functioning is never threatened, but rather the quality of their shop floor leadership's decision making and problem solving abilities enhanced;

☐ customers and other organisations start noticing the change in favour of QCs and national and international recognition is received;

☐ typical problems that are addressed include material and equipment, work procedures, safety and communications;

☐ an alternative to theoretical conventions/seminars is launched in the form of a one-day open air ('Rand Show type') event where all teams, customers and suppliers come together and practically demonstrate innovations;

☐ a variety of payback incentives are introduced as a part of Eskom's performance management system. These include team bonuses, a suggestion scheme, manager's awards and performance-based bonuses. Employees start reaping the benefit of improved quality and productivity;

☐ Eskom launches its 'electricity for all' programme to ensure that all South Africans are to get the benefit of electricity. QCs are very much involved in this process which requires innovation and extensive interaction with customers;

☐ the results of the programme of employee involvement through quality circles include improved quality of work life, better customer service, improved safety indices, new inventions/technology (one device saved R6-million a year), improved working procedures (work smarter), reduced wastage and enhanced productivity, improved literacy and numeracy, greater labour force harmony, cultural barriers falling down, leadership development and 'black advancement', more respect and teamwork, and higher level decision making by employees (part of the company family);

☐ the programme is currently enjoying massive growth in terms of employee participation levels and Eskom is assisting many other organisations and customers to do the same.

In summary, Eskom (Durban) has started the journey towards a culture that reflects entrepreneurship and democracy. The quality road is a difficult one but the commitment towards a new Eskom that will maximise the value of its products and services to South Africa is, in Eskom's view, very strong.

Johannesburg Consolidated Investment Company

*How the measurement of organisational climate and the use of a
team building intervention improved working relationships and
bottom line results on a mine*

This case study was conducted on one of the Group's mines over the
two-year period 1990-92, and is an indication of the benefits of a well
planned process to an organisation.

Teams who operate effectively contribute meaningfully to the
achievement of organisational goals. In teams everyone participates, objectives are clear and understood, listening takes place and effective action
is taken. Team development assists in achieving goals where there is a felt
need to improve some basic condition or process and solve problems.
Problems such as loss of production, increased grievances and complaints,
hostility and conflict, lack of involvement, increased costs and others have
a negative effect on output processed and negatively affect the wealth
creation capacity of the organisation.

Measurement of the climate of organisations assists in identifying
issues which need correction and in establishing the basis for the revitali-
sation process, which starts by improving team work. A questionnaire
followed by interviews is a suitable instrument for measuring climate.

The organisational development intervention concentrated on climate, process, team building and bottom-line performance.

The case study

The intervention began with analysis of organisational climate using
relevant questionnaires and follow-up interviews with employees to diag-
nose the situation. This took place on the mine in 1990. Following on from
this, feedback was given to mine management on the findings of the
climate survey. Inter alia, the following critical issues were regarded by
mine management as being the main areas of concern:

☐ communication, conflict handling, team building;
☐ production;
☐ community life.

After the feedback presentations, heads of departments made the following
suggestions:

☐ build and create team spirit;
☐ promote problem solving groups (PSGs);
☐ practical participative management;
☐ update mine standards;
☐ continue with management by objectives (MBO) to lower levels;
☐ make more use of supervisors;
☐ introduce new mining methods;
☐ cost awareness education;
☐ open door policy;
☐ eliminate dead stocks (stores);
☐ streamline buying system.

The JCI Organisation Development Unit (OD Unit) became very involved on-mine in assisting with the team building process. A team building programme (two-day course) was designed form literature. Thereafter, employees from departmental head down to foremen level attended the programme. Apart from the formal input on team building, the mine manager continued with consultative meetings, communication meetings and PSGs. He and his top team put in considerable effort to redress problems that were identified in the climate survey. The comprehensive and detailed climate survey report was used extensively by managers to assist in identifying problem areas and taking appropriate action involving their people. The team building intervention facilitated the overall team building process on the mine, and assisted the mine manager to achieve his results. Results achieved through the process are twofold:

☐ improvements in attitude towards the work environment (climate results); and
☐ improvements in bottom-line results.

Improvements in climate

Fourteen factors were measured in the climate questionnaire. Pre-intervention results were obtained in 1990 (ie before any action was taken by the mine to solve problems). These are presented as standard percentile scores. A follow-up survey was conducted in 1992 after the team building intervention and action taken by mine management to improve results. The table shows the results and indicates improvement in climate on all factors measured.

Factor	Pre-Intervention Standard Score 1990	Post-Intervention Standard Score 1992	Significance Level of Difference (Probability)
Decisions	56	65	0.2056
Organisation Structure	59	72	0.1416
Role Clarity	50	66	0.0287*
Standards	56	66	0.0454*
Conflict Handling	44	56	0.0481*
Supervisory Effectiveness	50	56	0.1558
Communication	52	58	0.2557
Team Building	50	63	0.0202*
Responsibility	47	53	0.2276
Reward	52	59	0.0519*
Job Satisfaction	46	53	0.1775
Job Tension	50	47	0.7562
Propensity to Leave	55	42	0.0193*
Contribution to Profit	52	67	0.0043*

* Highly significant improvements. All other factors have improved.

Improvements in hard results

The following are improvements in hard results for the period 1990 to 1992:

☐ number of employees remained constant;
☐ tonnes produced (average per month indexed)

June 1989	100
June 1990	106
June 1991	117
June 1992	120

Overall increase in production: 20%;
☐ cost per tonne produced increased only 4% per annum;

☐ profitability ranking of the three shafts on the mine compared to 12 other shafts in the group:

Profitability ranking per shaft		
	1990	1992
Shaft A	10	1
Shaft B	11	2
Shaft C	12	4

The mine could not have achieved the results without the dedication, drive and sincerity of the mine manager. The OD Unit acted as a catalyst to help the mine manager bring about change. The following are the significant characteristics of the mine manager, who made the changes in climate and results possible. These characteristics were established during interviews with mine employees:

☐ practical mining experience;
☐ management by walking about (MBWA) – regular visits;
☐ listens supportively (action);
☐ open minded – doesn't take things personally;
☐ controls costs;
☐ sets objectives, delegates, follows up;
☐ systematically ensures critical blockages removed;
☐ counsels subordinates;
☐ promotes teamwork top down;
☐ not charismatic, unlike the norm;
☐ medium to long term thinker.

Conclusion

The project was successful. The mine manager admits that the help of the OD Unit was very useful in helping him and his top team gain insight into mine problems and assisting them with the appropriate change process. It was a joint effort between the OD Unit and the mine personnel.

There is little doubt that if problems can be diagnosed properly, and presented to management sensibly and sensitively, a planned strategy can be developed to bring about desired change as this case study has shown.

4

The interface between business and community during the transition

The RoBiT discussion sessions identified the interface between business and the broader community as a key challenge facing business during the transition. A stable environment for future economic growth will depend on curbing violence, crime and poverty, and the private sector has a crucial role to play in addressing these problems. A recent Business Marketing Intelligence survey estimated that South African corporations spend R840 million on social upliftment programmes. This significant amount has the potential to impact strongly on development and growth.

There has been a trend in the community-business interface to move away from 'cheque book charity' towards greater involvement of company personnel and community empowerment in making development projects sustainable. At the same time, the private sector sometimes lacks vision and a policy framework within which corporate social investment (CSI) and community involvement can contribute to sustainable development and economic growth. Comparatively small amounts are spent on job creation and enterprise development schemes as opposed to straight-forward charity.

On the basis of the RoBiT discussion sessions and lessons from the past and present, CBM drew up the following guidelines which offer a framework for the interface between business and community during the transition:

Aim for sustainable development through

- ☐ partnerships between companies and communities;
- ☐ building institutions that will outlast company involvement;
- ☐ empowerment of communities to manage and reproduce development;
- ☐ community control.

Process determines the product.

- ☐ Correct process may cause some delays but it will also ensure that community organisations and representatives fully understand and support a particular project. Correct process will allow a focus on community needs and build the capacity of individuals to manage development.

Commitment and resources.

- ☐ Business must be prepared to make a long term commitment to communities and devote the necessary resources to projects if its interface with communities is to be successful.

Economic growth.

- ☐ Business has a direct interest in supporting projects that will stimulate the economy and create jobs.

Focus.

- ☐ During the transition business needs to focus on key obstacles. The combating of violence and voter education will be key issues in the coming year. The installation of a legitimate interim government is the most important underlying goal during the transition.

Developing a private sector approach.

- ☐ The private sector needs to develop policy frameworks and approaches for its work in the development sector. In addition, business needs to be well organised and coherent in its participation in the various co-operative processes and forums that have been set up.

Networking and sharing of resources.

- ☐ Given the difficult economic times, the RoBiT discussion sessions identified a need to network between companies, thereby avoiding duplication and obtaining maximum benefit from scarce resources.

A selection of case studies, which is not exhaustive in any way, is annexed to this chapter to illustrate practically the approach of some companies and groups to these problems.

Chapter Four

The interface between business and community during the transition

Business leaders involved in the RoBiT discussion sessions agreed that the interface between business and the wider community was a key challenge facing South African business during the transition. They agreed that South Africa needed symbols of success in deprived communities. The private sector, it was argued, should carefully consider how its scarce resources in this field could be utilised effectively and how lessons learnt could be shared.

This chapter outlines a possible framework for a business approach to the community-business interface and makes practical suggestions for action.

A private sector perspective on community projects and development

A stable environment for future economic growth in South Africa will depend on curbing violence, crime and poverty. The private sector has become increasingly aware that well-educated employees with houses, electricity and secure family lives will be more productive and effective than employees living in squalor and shacks.

The private sector has a critical role in contributing to the development needs of South Africa, particularly during the transition. Government has only recently started to address the development backlog arising from decades of apartheid policies. In many areas government development projects have been discredited. Urgent problems such as housing shortages, the education crisis, unemployment and violence threaten to wreck hopes of a stable and peaceful transition. Those who were discriminated against under apartheid have high socio-economic expectations of a future government. Development programmes that create symbols of success and meaningfully combat poverty in depressed communities may temper the inevitable anger and frustration that will flow from the gap between delivery and expectation that a new government will face.

South African business spending on social investment programmes is arguably one of the highest in the world, and yet the image of South African business as uncaring and profit-hungry persists. In addition, many businesses have felt frustrated by the lack of visible success from their social investment programmes.

Over the past few years, thinking within business has matured regarding the nature and role of business involvement in socio-economic development. Some of the most important lessons in this regard are:

☐ the need for focused and targeted programmes aimed at building symbols of success;
☐ the need to move away from 'cheque book charity' to active partnerships between business and community;
☐ increased community control over projects;
☐ the need to aim at self-sufficiency and replicability.

Social investment can be seen as a 'two-way street' in which there are benefits for both communities and business. Businesses can build positive profiles in the black community and, through involving personnel in community development projects, develop staff with an understanding of community problems. Through contact with business, community organisations can begin to understand the constraints that business operates within, and the way that business is managed.

Current involvement in social investment

The Business Marketing and Intelligence estimate of R840 million spent on CSI during 1990/91 (which excludes trust funds) reveals the importance that business attaches to CSI and the potential impact that CSI spending can have on development (see diagram 1).

All too often, however, CSI departments are understaffed, overworked and crisis driven. In some instances, CSI departments appear woefully ill-equipped to deal with the challenge of moving beyond 'cheque book' approaches to CSI.

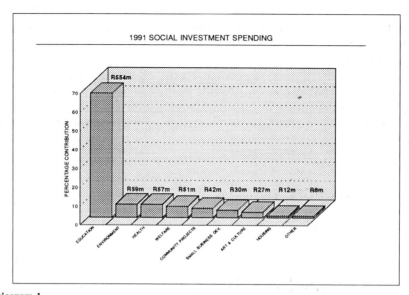

Diagram 1

According to a CBM survey of member companies conducted in 1990, companies allocate CSI funds in the following way:

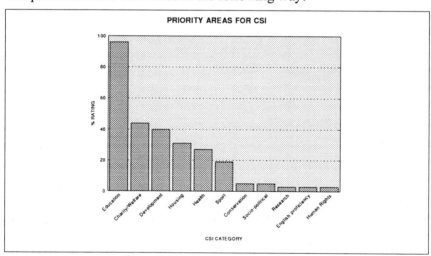

Diagram 2

Education is clearly one of the greatest areas of concern for the private sector. According to the CBM survey, 77 per cent of businesses polled are active in education projects, 96 per cent see it as a priority area, 62 per cent provide literacy programmes in-house and a further 72 per cent provide in-house management and skills training programmes. Twenty-two per cent of the sample indicated that they wished to mesh education initiatives with other companies.

The survey showed that 44 per cent of the sample funds were contributed to charity concerns. While the private sector will always be a major contributor to charity, this fairly high percentage raises the issue of the effectiveness of CSI spending in contributing to sustainable development.

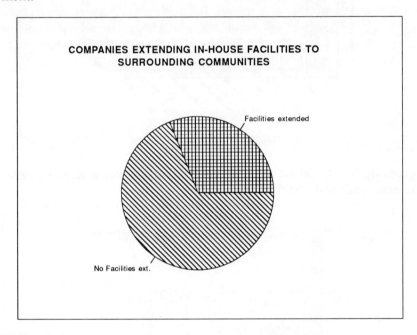

Diagram 3

Thirty-one per cent of the sample extend in-house facilities to the communities surrounding the factories (see diagram 3 above). The Department of Health argues that efforts to extend health clinic services to at least families of employees is an essential component of rationalising expenditure between public and private health agencies.

In addition, 72 per cent of the sample indicated that they had management and skills training programmes. The potential exists for business to lend support to capacity building and community empowerment programmes through, for example, training community leaders in basic management, financial control and planning.

Forty per cent of the survey sample did not discuss their CSI programmes with unions or communities. This has been widely criticised by trade unions and community organisations. CSI programmes set up in consultation with community organisations are more likely to be focused on real and identified needs, and more likely to involve community co-operation and involvement leading to empowerment rather than dependency.

Business has become increasingly involved in the National Peace Accord, recognising the urgency of curbing violence in creating a stable political and economic environment. Business has in many instances been able to play the role of an even-handed facilitator. One of the problems identified, however, is that where business acts as a facilitator, this constrains the extent to which its own interests are represented. In addition, business representatives often lack the skills to act as community facilitators and negotiators. CBM has organised a number of training and strategising sessions in this regard.

By and large, however, business has responded to community needs in a reactive manner. The business sector, largely because of its competitive and heterogeneous nature, has not formed a vision of how development can contribute to the creation of an environment for economic growth and increased productivity.

Guidelines for the business-community interface during the transition

Drawing on the RoBiT discussion sessions and lessons from the past and present, CBM has drawn up the following guidelines:

- Aim for sustainable development through
  * partnerships between companies and communities
  * building institutions to outlast company involvement
  * empowerment of communities and community control
- Process determines the product
- Business must commit energy and resources
- Support projects that encourage economic growth
- Focus spending to smooth the transition and lay the basis for a new South Africa
- Develop a private sector approach and organise for effective business input into processes
- Network and sharing of resources for maximum impact.

Aim for sustainable development

While the transitional period may demand urgent responses to community needs, business involvement in community projects should aim at sustainable development. Sustainable development can be built in the following ways:

Partnerships

Partnerships entail a two-way relationship in which the private sector goes beyond merely writing cheques but becomes integrally involved by allocating human resources to projects, assisting organisations with implementation of projects and building the skills of individuals in communities.

Partnerships can be found in a variety of forms, from business involvement in local peace accord structures, to joint initiatives such as the Soweto Education Co-ordinating Committee-CBM partnership, detailed in the case studies attached to this chapter.

The advantages of local level partnerships are as follows:

☐ relationships of trust are built between individuals;
☐ business gains an understanding of community needs and dynamics;
☐ communities gain an understanding of business needs and constraints;
☐ instead of responding to ad hoc appeals for assistance during crisis, business is in a two-way ongoing relationship with the community;
☐ skills can be transferred to communities and community organisations using existing company resources;
☐ local communities can be built through co-operation between all the major players.

Some of the lessons from the past are detailed below:

☐ all the major political and social groupings must be drawn in. The exclusion of a particular political grouping may exacerbate conflict within the community;
☐ the ground rules setting out what each party can expect from the partnership must be clear, and the financial and human resource commitment spelt out. If these issues are not confronted, expectations may be dashed, damaging company credibility;
☐ sustainable development depends on community organisations achieving the capacity to control and direct development. If this aspect is not

systematically attended to, the private sector is seen as a never-ending source of funds and a dependent relationship is created;

☐ the commitment and patience required on the part of the private sector to establish lasting and productive partnerships between the private sector and community is immense, but the benefits of successful partnerships far outweigh the frustrations.

Institution building

One of the most damaging legacies of apartheid involves the almost total breakdown of structures and institutions in black communities. Development in these communities will only be sustainable if the institutions of ordinary life are systematically rebuilt.

In the long term, a democratically elected government at national and local level is essential for the reconstruction of our society, but in the interim democratic and accountable institutions must be built to meet community needs.

Communities are often represented by organisations that are organisationally weak, lacking adequate resources and professional skills. Business involvement should address these needs at the practical level of physical resources and with financial and managerial skills.

Community Development Trusts are a more formalised method of drawing together various interest groups in a trust structure, allowing community interests to be represented while drawing on the expertise and resources of more resource-rich groups such as private sector developers and local authorities.

Empowerment and community control

Development that aims at empowerment must include an educational component, enabling community representatives to understand and if necessary criticise development plans. Consultation without genuine empowerment is window dressing and will not deliver the benefits of a truly consultative process. Consultation implies a willingness to change plans if necessary, and will start by identifying community needs rather than rubber-stamping plans that are already finalised.

Process

Correct process will ensure that community needs are focused on, that community control is emphasised and that the capacity of individuals is built.

Process and painstaking rounds of consultations can be time consuming, but are likely to be worth it in the end. Many projects have failed or become white elephants because of weak process. While one should seek to avoid unnecessary stalling, a patient approach that covers all the bases may produce longer lasting results.

Co-operative processes between different interest groups have emerged in a number of different sectors such as housing (the National Housing Forum), electricity, water and sanitation. At a more general level, the National Economic Forum and various regional economic and development forums have emerged.

Business is represented in each of these forums and is seen as an important stakeholder. It is in these forums that the need for business to develop its own policy approach comes to the fore.

Commitment and resources

If business is going to make any real difference to the lives of the poor, a real commitment to community involvement backed with adequate resources is needed. The hurdles in community development are numerous and long lasting commitment is essential if business is to build its credibility. CSI departments are in most instances the driving forces behind the business-community interface. These departments complain of being inadequately staffed and crisis driven.

A genuine commitment to real change requires allocating the necessary resources or accessing them from other actors such as other businesses, development agencies and government.

Economic growth

Current CSI expenditure could have a real impact on development. Business has a direct interest in developing policies and projects that will boost the economy and create jobs. While support for charity concerns is necessary in the current climate, the private sector can support and undertake initiatives that will offer economic growth and longer term solutions to poverty. Job creation projects and projects that kickstart local economies will be critical building blocks for future economic growth.

Development projects need to be evaluated in this light and each project aimed at achieving these goals. This need not entail massive spending or bureaucratic structures (see, for example, the Get Ahead case study at the end of this chapter).

Focus during the transition and beyond

Spending needs to be focused on key needs. During the RoBiT work sessions, peace was raised as a key focus. Delegates pointed out that without peace, a negotiated settlement could be jeopardised, undermining any basis for economic growth.

During the transition the most obvious underlying focus for business effort is on the installation of a legitimate government. Business needs to identify impediments to this goal and act to remove or assist in removing these obstacles.

The absence of a legitimate government has seriously hampered the implementation of development plans. Development agencies around the country have tales of woe regarding inability to spend funds allocated to specific projects because of 'political conflict'. Furthermore, CSI spending needs to be focused on those whose needs are greatest – the poor.

As national elections based on universal franchise draw closer, business will have a responsibility to tackle the issue of voter education. A free and fair election will depend on the extent to which millions of South Africans who have never voted before, exercise their vote without fear of intimidation.

Developing a private sector approach

Business is increasingly being called upon to represent its interests in a variety of forums and co-operative processes.

Business is not, however, a homogeneous group. It is intensely competitive, yet does constitute an identifiable interest group. Other interest groups in forums and processes will often caucus their positions and have clear ideas on agendas and priorities. Business will have to consider how it can ensure that its interests are represented. Business organisations will have to develop mandating procedures and mechanisms for keeping their constituents up to date and supportive of decisions taken.

Community involvement is a two-way street. If business is to obtain the full benefit of community involvement, it will have to develop its own policies and approach to development in the transition.

Networking and sharing of resources

The RoBiT discussion sessions identified a need to network within busi-ness to avoid duplication and obtain maximum benefit.

Some smaller companies felt that they did not have the resources to initiate their own projects but would be eager to contribute in conjunction with others.

Networking was also seen as important as a way of sharing experiences and evaluating the contribution business was making.

A specific focus on peace

While peace is only one area of the community-business interface, business leaders have frequently raised the need for greater involvement in the peace process. Questions about the best way to make this contribution have also been raised.

What follows are a set of guideline on how business can contribute within the framework of the Peace Accord. The Mpumalanga case study at the end of this chapter adds practical value to these guidelines:

☐ *Make a conscious decision to enter the peace process and accept the full implications thereof.* Becoming a partner to the peace process at local level is a serious decision. Recognise that this is a time consuming exercise demanding of human, physical and financial resources. Allocate people to spend time on the process. Be prepared to open the doors of your company to those involved in the peace process for meetings.

☐ *Involve the trade unions in the process at the start.* The content of the Peace Accord should not be seen as automatically desirable to the workforce and surrounding communities. Trade union and community leaders should be involved from the outset in examining the best way to expedite the process. They will know the lay of the land best in the communities and should direct the setting of priorities.

☐ *Approach the regional dispute resolution committee, organisations like CBM or local business chambers for guidance.* In the absence of a regional dispute resolution committee, approach the National Peace Secretariat. Discuss the process you envisage and which actors need to be involved. Consult all actors and determine who should facilitate and mediate the process if not business itself. If appropriate, apply for status as a local dispute resolution committee. This gives the process legal and judicial effect.

☐ *Involve all actors in the process.* Ensure that an inclusive process is followed. All political parties, community groups, establishment organisations and development agencies should be approached. But the political parties will be the first port of call and will need to give the lead as to who else to involve. Be prepared to fund and facilitate separate meetings of political parties to consider their approach to the process before bringing them into a multilateral forum.

☐ *Back the process with resources and determine a programme for reconstruction.* Peace without development in the longer term will only frustrate agreements. Examine how to give momentum to local level development and reconstruction in line with the regional reconstruction committees. The parties and communities should direct reconstruction priorities. View this partnership as a long term and sustainable effort at uplifting community life.

☐ *Popularise the Peace Accord and communicate progress.* In liaison with other actors in the process, use the company resources to popularise the Accord (for example joint meetings with employees, use of company billboards and newsletters, etc). Communicate progress through the press if other parties agree to this.

☐ *Commit to the process.* This is a medium to long term commitment which will have its ups and downs. Do not view your involvement as short term or else surrounding communities are likely to become bitter at being deserted.

Conclusion

The case studies which follow are an indication of just how much business has already contributed to the area of development and peace. But the need is endless and requires even greater business input and coherence. The guidelines in this chapter and lessons gleaned from the case studies should help to ensure that scarce business resources are dedicated to this end as optimally as possible.

Premier's Social Investment Council

One of the few CSI programmes to have consulted with worker representatives is Premier's Social Investment Council. Approximately four years ago it was decided that the council should include equal representatives of workers and management. The council's task is to:

☐ decide on funding applications;
☐ offer guidance and administrative assistance to projects;
☐ follow up projects;
☐ intervene where necessary.

Trade union representatives are elected to the eight different regional councils and the National Executive of the council, and have made a significant impact on CSI spending at Premier. The chair of the council rotates annually between management and workers.

The various projects' needs are carefully assessed and cash hand-outs are the last resort. Donations in kind of Premier products, equipment or assistance of expertise located in the company may be more appropriate.

Representatives on the Social Investment Council and other company personnel tend to get involved in the various projects while encouraging communities to provide 'sweat equity'.

In Pongola, where a Premier cotton mill is situated, the local community approached Premier for funds for a pre-school. The worker representatives initiated a community building committee and a brick machine was purchased. The community is now producing bricks for the building, acquiring skills and significantly reducing the costs of the project.

Premier's school feeding scheme aimed to be feeding 50 000 school children by the end of 1992. The scheme is run from the local level and worker representatives are responsible for selecting schools and ensuring community participation in the project. Worker representatives pointed out that in a scheme such as this, they had to consider what effect the scheme would have on the livelihood of hawkers selling food outside schools.

The input of worker representatives in the Social Investment Councils has proved to be invaluable in assessing community needs and providing assistance to projects.

The Get Ahead Foundation

Get Ahead was started in the early 1980s to provide start-up capital for small businesses. To date it has granted 12 000 loans with a book value of R10 million. It processes 1 000 loans a month, creating 12 000 to 15 000 jobs a year. There are a number of aspects to Get Ahead's work which provide pointers to businesses wishing to get involved in community projects. Get Ahead is very willing to work with companies on projects that they may wish to finance or initiate.

Using traditional financing vehicles

Get Ahead utilises the stokvel system to:

☐ provide collateral for its loans;
☐ act as a point of interface with Get Ahead's field workers;
☐ enforce loan repayment through peer pressure.

Essentially, a potential borrower is advised to find approximately eight other borrowers, who, once approved as borrowers, then form a stokvel. No individual collateral is required. The loans are small, ranging from R100 to R5 000. The stokvel will operate as an ordinary stokvel but in addition to the monthly stokvel payment, borrowers will pay their Get Ahead installment. The Get Ahead field worker is able to collect all payments at the monthly stokvel meeting and deal with any problems that may have arisen. The stokvel group also undergoes basic business skills training.

The system seems to have been successful with only a six per cent bad debt figure and 8 000 jobs created. Get Ahead also operates a more formal business loans programme.

Get Ahead works with existing organisations in training and instruct them in the methods employed by Get Ahead.

Consistent support and training

Through trade and 'matchmaker' fairs, small businesses are introduced to bigger businesses and township markets.

Get Ahead also approaches big corporations to support these small and emerging businesses through sub-contracting.

Business seminars using the skills and venues of bigger corporations, on the spot advice and joint ventures with business schools all aim at ensuring that businesses started with Get Ahead finance will succeed.

Projects that create jobs

One of the most creative projects in this category has been the 'Car Wash Project'. Unemployed people are taught how to wash cars and mini-bus taxis. They are also given elementary instruction in business skills such as costing and record keeping.

The Get Ahead approach is aimed at fulfilling community needs as identified by community people. It uses simple techniques and methods that are familiar to communities.

The Lugobe school project

CBM in Natal has networked various companies and organisations together in a project which uses a school in Umbumbulu as its focal point.

The Lugobe school has 650 standard nine and ten children, with 750 adults being taught in the evenings. The Urban Foundation is presently building two new classrooms. The school is a focal point in the community and through a series of consultative meetings involving CBM member companies and development agencies it was determined that the school could be a starting point for development activities.

Through networking a variety of sources of development funds, the following projects were identified:

- [ ] electrification;
- [ ] provision of school equipment and teacher upgrading;
- [ ] the sinking of a borehole and the selling of water through the school to pay for electricity;
- [ ] a hot-shower shop to provide income for the school.

CBM was also able to link this development initiative to the Peace Accord. Now that the initial facilitation phase is over CBM will endeavour to partner the school with member companies.

The Soweto Education Initiative

The Soweto Education Initiative is an example of the evolution of partnership between the Soweto Education Co-ordinating Committee (SECC) and CBM member companies. SECC is an organisation representing parents, students and teachers concerned about the crisis in education in Soweto.

The partnership between SECC and CBM members aimed 'to develop mutual trust in a process aimed at restoring hope for the education system, and its material improvement'.

The partnership has gone through a number of phases:

☐ introducing CBM members and others to the education crisis during a bus tour of Soweto;
☐ initiating meetings with the DET and starting to play a facilitative role;
☐ engaging in practical activities such as textbook delivery and auditing of school records;
☐ planning for the future.

The Soweto Education Initiative has reflected many of the benefits and frustrations of a partnership approach. The initiative has had a fundamental impact on education in Soweto. From a situation where the DET and the SECC were unable to work together, the relationship now largely occurs on a bilateral basis without the need for the presence of a third party facilitator.

One of the victories of the facilitative process was the delivery of textbooks to Soweto in a joint process. SECC officials escorted delivery vehicles into Soweto ensuring that the correct textbooks were delivered.

In addition, the committee has run a campaign to assist matric students with extra classes. Throughout the year individuals within the SECC have improved their managerial and financial skills and have also developed as adept negotiators. These victories have been crucial to maintaining the credibility of the process amongst the parties. The process has, however, had many setbacks:

Resources: CBM members were called upon to dig into their pockets on a number of occasions. These expenses were not foreseen and not budgeted for. The process involved many long and sometimes tedious meetings, and individual business people and busy chief executives found it difficult to devote the necessary time and energy.

Capacity: At the beginning of the process the SECC had very few resources and members had to assist in this regard. Individuals similarly lacked managerial and other skills. This led to a degree of dependency on the CBM team. There was no clearly structured programme to address the needs of the organisation although through the process, all concerned, *including businesspeople*, have acquired new skills and insights.

Partisanship: At the same time as CBM members were assisting in the facilitation of process, they were also supporting one of the parties involved. This caused some initial tension with DET structures but after discussions this problem was solved.

The involvement of CBM members in the Soweto Education Initiative has not been without problems. Yet without commitment to the process and a willingness to go through the bad patches, the parties would never have been able to achieve so much and go so far along the road towards a 'normal' education system in Soweto.

Mpumalanga

Mpumalanga was built in the mid-1960s to house the many thousands of people who – as a result of decentralisation policy – had come to work in Hammarsdale. Mpumalanga has a population of about 50 000 official residents, with a further 100 000 in the surrounding rural area. Half the population is under 15 years of age and unemployment is estimated to be in the region of 50 per cent or higher. Infrastructure is sparse.

In 1986, violence broke out in the Natal Midlands and quickly spread to Mpumalanga. What had been a peaceful town become the most violent of towns, soon gaining the title of 'Little Beirut'.

Faced with near anarchy, absenteeism, stayaways and death or harm to their workers, black and white local business intervened in September 1989 in the Mpumalanga peace initiative at the request of shop stewards.

Peace efforts went through ups and downs, being influenced by local and national events. When the ANC was unbanned, for example, violence broke out. When the ANC and IFP signed a national peace accord in January 1991, this impacted positively on local peace initiatives.

Mpumalanga has experienced a major transformation. Parents who support different political parties are serving together on school committees. Youth from both parties are playing soccer and other sports together; slowly the society is becoming normalised. 'But', says Steve Simpson, Industrial Relations Personnel Manager for South African Nylon Spinners in Hammarsdale, 'if we want peace to become a permanent feature of Mpumalanga ... there is much to be done. Communities such as Mpumalanga need support and reward for their peace initiatives.' It is in this light that the focus has shifted to include reconstruction.

The Joint Working Group for Natal, led by the ANC's Jacob Zuma and IFP's Frank Mdlalose, has established a trust fund named the Peace and Reconstruction Foundation Trust. The local Mpumalanga Peace Initiative Group, made up of ANC and IFP members and industrialists, has formed a committee called the Mpumalanga Reconstruction Co-ordinating Committee (MRCC).

This committee aims to liaise with the community to establish and agree upon priorities for the rehabilitation of Mpumalanga, negotiate with organisations such as the Urban Foundation and draw up proposals for the Joint Working Group to consider and approve for funding. The committee's other role is to monitor progress of work done and approve accounts for payments by the Trust. Two projects currently underway involve

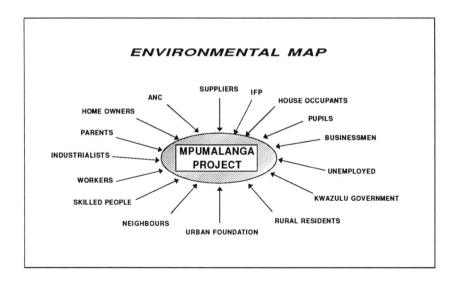

ENVIRONMENTAL MAP

repairs to the four high schools damaged during the violence, as the building of a community hall.

Other projects needing urgent attention are the repairs to all other schools and some 1 500 houses damaged by the unrest. The housing project is undoubtedly the most expensive and emotional. The best way to address the issue is currently being debated in depth. The success of the reconstruction process is dependent on many factors, but if it succeeds, it will act as a model for others to follow.

Critical lessons learnt

☐ the timing of intervention is of paramount importance; the community has to signal it has had enough and is ready for assistance. Just as a marriage guidance counsellor has to wait for at least one of the married partners to seek help before intervening, so too a mediator has to wait for the community to request help. For Mpumalanga industrialists it was the shop stewards who signaled the time was right;

☐ wherever possible, the mediator should broaden the intervention base. White industrialists did this by involving the black businessmen. It had a positive effect on the community, and allowed far more information to be gathered and a better understanding of the complexities;

☐ it is important to focus on local leaders. They are the people who are feeling the pain. They are also the ones who will eventually have to work out solutions for their area. It is, however, of utmost importance to keep national leaders informed and solicit their support;

- knowing who to initially make contact with is very important. The 'gatekeeper' of the organisation either allows you in or discredits your attempts;
- at the outset, it is important to be open and honest about the reasons for involvement. The business agenda was made very clear right at the beginning, namely the survival of the business sector;
- it is key to caucus separately with each party; business helped to prepare both sides for their initial face-to-face encounter, which was then not emotional and confrontational;
- the first meeting is very important, and preparation is therefore essential. Helping the parties to determine their agenda and list priorities, and highlighting common ground were major factors that led to the signing of the cease-fire agreement at the end of their very first meeting;
- it was important to launder the language at meetings in order to reduce emotional outbursts. By clarifying and rephrasing provocative statements, meaningful dialogue and understanding were achieved;
- the future was concentrated on. The past is history and nothing can change that. Meetings become very heated and unproductive when people dwell on apportioning blame and seeking retribution;
- efforts were made to minimise interference by politicians and other groups trying to help. Business had to meet and explain the need to support the process, but adopt a low profile, to such groups. It confuses the community when there are too many actors in the process. It also questions the credentials of the main players;
- a low profile with regard to the news media was maintained whenever possible, to avoid the risk of being branded opportunists. Personal statements can be misinterpreted and have serious consequences on the mediator's impartial status. It was practice, wherever possible, to issue joint statements;
- on occasions, one or other of the parties wanted to meet with business separately. To maintain its impartial status, business made it clear that everything discussed would be shared with the other players and made sure this was done;
- the holding of frequent meetings, especially in the very early stages, meant that problems were addressed quickly. Continuous monitoring of the situation is vital;
- business accepted that progress would be slow. The leaders have a very difficult role, and if they do not have the support of all sections of their constituencies, agreements concluded become difficult, if not impossible, to implement;

☐ it was important to accept that new faces would appear from time to time at meetings. Sometimes this was because of a change in leadership within sections of the constituencies, and sometimes out of curiosity by some to see what was going on. If the parties were happy for them to be there, then the newcomers' credentials were not challenged;

☐ business had to accept that meetings would not always start on time, and that people would arrive late. This was not because of disrespect or lack of interest, but in most instances due to transport and communication problems. Very few telephones are available in the township and transport is erratic;

☐ business needed to exercise patience and not rush meetings to show that they were sincere and not wanting to take sides. Blocking someone from making a statement could be viewed in this way. Most meetings tend to be of long duration, relative to the issues being discussed, mainly because it is customary for people openly to show support or otherwise for the subject being debated, even if it merely means restating a viewpoint already expressed by others;

☐ meetings were often postponed at the eleventh hour. Sometimes, other issues arose, such as splits in the ranks on one or the other side, that required the leaders' attention, before being able to proceed further with peace talks;

☐ it was important as mediators to be well informed and up-to-date on all incidents in the area which could affect the peace process. Knowing what was going on showed that business cared and was taking an interest;

☐ it was important for the businesspeople to familiarise themselves with the names of all the areas, important streets, nicknames given to them, as well as with individuals and groups. It helps not only to understand what is being discussed, but also to demonstrate to all that you are knowledgeable about what is going on. People automatically accept you more readily if you have a knowledge of their environment.

(This case study is drawn from *Track Two*, 1, May 1992, where Steve Simpson, Industrial Relations Personnel Manager for South African Nylon Spinners in Hammarsdale, chronicled the Mpumalanga experience.)

The case of the National Housing Forum

In November 1991, a wide range of national players involved in housing met in Johannesburg to discuss a process to formulate an inclusive national housing policy. Out of this meeting the National Housing Forum (NHF), formally launched on 31 August 1992, was established.

The NHF is made up of representatives from labour, business, political parties, civics and development agencies. The government was initially involved, but withdrew, believing that Codesa was a more appropriate structure for such discussion. While government is not a formal participant in the NHF, there is regular bilateral contact between the NHF and government. The aim of the NHF is to formulate a set

of short term strategies, medium and long term plans and policy frameworks for the housing sector, on a basis that includes all who have a national contribution to the housing sector, and on a basis which allows maximum participation by the general public through the components of the forum.

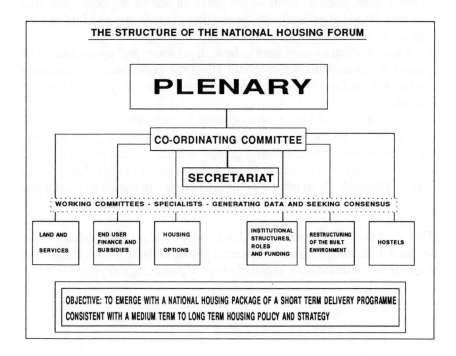

THE STRUCTURE OF THE NATIONAL HOUSING FORUM

PLENARY

CO-ORDINATING COMMITTEE

SECRETARIAT

WORKING COMMITTEES - SPECIALISTS - GENERATING DATA AND SEEKING CONSENSUS

| LAND AND SERVICES | END USER FINANCE AND SUBSIDIES | HOUSING OPTIONS | INSTITUTIONAL STRUCTURES, ROLES AND FUNDING | RESTRUCTURING OF THE BUILT ENVIRONMENT | HOSTELS |

OBJECTIVE: TO EMERGE WITH A NATIONAL HOUSING PACKAGE OF A SHORT TERM DELIVERY PROGRAMME CONSISTENT WITH A MEDIUM TERM TO LONG TERM HOUSING POLICY AND STRATEGY

The business sector is represented in the NHF in five different areas: employers (Saccola), end user finance sector (Mortgage Lenders Association), contractual savings sector (Life Officers Association), the construction industry (the Construction Consortium) and the materials suppliers industry (the Materials Suppliers Consortium). Business co-ordinates and discusses its inputs into the NHF through an informal 'business caucus' which meets twice a month. In addition, each sector of business discusses its own involvement and strategies in its relevant organisations. For the materials industry and the construction industry, specific 'paper' organisations had to be formed.

Throughout the short history of the NHF, business has had to respond to the challenge of strong and organised representatives from other sectors of the NHF such as the political parties or the trade union federations. This challenge forced business to become one of the most organised and effective lobbies within the forum.

An example of the fruits of this level of organisation and common and separate strategising was seen at the NHF's two day internal strategic workshop, where careful and co-ordinated presentations from the business sector greatly enhanced the level and focus of discussion and debate.

The effective co-ordination and structuring of business input into the NHF has proved to be a very demanding task for those members of the business community involved in the forum. However, a strong and prepared business lobby within the discussions and decision making of the NHF has proved invaluable, both for business and for the process more generally.

Murray and Roberts' Sunflower Projects

Murray and Roberts started to train unemployed people in 1985. Training moved into deprived communities to enable the unemployed within those communities to uplift themselves by acquiring skills whilst through the process providing sorely needed facilities. These became known as Sunflower Projects.

The initiative started in Natal, but now has projects nationwide. Sunflower's mission, simply stated, is to uplift deprived communities through the provision of education and training. Sunflower's success lies in its ability to provide an effective delivery mechanism for sustainable upliftment through creating a committed partnership with each community in which their involvement and participation are essential key components of the process.

Andrew Stewart, former MD of M&R Natal, and now full-time with Sunflower, comments that 'without community commitment, we would be wasting our time'. Typically, a community requests Sunflower's assistance. After needs have been clarified and funds secured, training commences on site. After basic skills have been learnt, trainees commence work on the community facilities under the guidance of their instructors. The formal building skills training is accredited by the Building Industries Training Board. A wide range of informal training is also provided including:

☐ dressmaking;
☐ knitting;
☐ hairdressing;
☐ leatherwork;
☐ vegetable gardening.

It soon became apparent that literacy and numeracy training was necessary and this has become an essential part of Sunflower Projects. This has been expanded to provide for a broad range of adult education through the Business Management Association.

Sunflower aims at making people self-sustaining, and entrepreneurial development has become an important aspect of its operation. The essence of Sunflower Projects involves

☐ community commitment and participation;

☐ empowerment through skills enhancement, literacy and adult education;
☐ entrepreneurial development;
☐ labour intensity;
☐ job creation.

This has enabled Sunflower to leave a legacy of viable wealth generating community facilities, skilled workers (including many women) and literate people. Pride and dignity are restored.

Sunflower helps communities enlist the support of public and corporate funders. A number of corporations, NGOs and aid agencies have 'adopted' specific Sunflower projects but there are still many projects held in abeyance until financial support can be found.

The vision of the programme is to cover the whole of Southern Africa and even beyond with sunflowers.

MANAGING CHANGE

Conclusion

It is very rare these days to find a businessperson questioning why business should play a role in transition. Many are already active and others question only how they can become involved or refine their involvement.

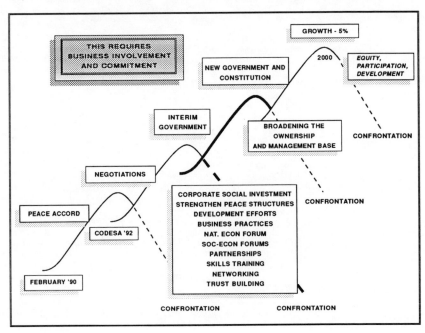

This book is a contribution to that debate. It is a recognition of the already very significant role of business in the South African transition, especially when comparisons are drawn with transitions elsewhere. But it also acknowledges the gaps and enormous challenges that business still needs to meet.

The four areas of focus – the macro-environment in transition; broadening the ownership and management base; effective and legitimate business practices in the transition; and the interface between business and community – are separate but integrated. Neglect of any one will influence the ability of South Africa to succeed in its search for a successful transition and for stability and progress thereafter. The diagram opposite illustrates how the concepts and strategies contained in this book are part of an holistic effort to help South African society in its search for peace, growth and democracy.

It is hoped that, in time to come, *MANAGING CHANGE* will have contributed to this quest for peace, democracy and economic progress.

Contact people and organisations

National Consultative Group of the Consultative Business Movement

COMPANY	DELEGATE
ABBEY HOLDINGS	J SCHAFFER
AECI	M SANDER
AA CORPORATION	M SPICER
ARGUS HOLDINGS	M HOFMEYR
BARLOW RAND	J HALL
CALTEX	J MCKENZIE
CBM	T ELOFF
DBSA	A LA GRANGE
ESKOM	G LINDEQUE
GENCOR	N STEENKAMP
GENTYRE	C TUTTON
JCI	K MAXWELL
MCCARTHY GROUP	B MCCARTHY
MUNICH RE-INS	E KAHLE
MURRAY & ROBERTS	D BRINK
NAMPAK	P CAMPBELL
NEDCOR	C LIEBENBERG
NORWICH LIFE	C DAVIES
PG BISON	A BAND
PG BISON	L COHEN
PREMIER GROUP	P WRIGHTON
SEGEFIN	D MASSON
SOUTHERN LIFE	N CHAPMAN
SOUTHERN LIFE	A VAN DER ZWAN
T&N HOLDINGS	MC PRETORIUS

COMPANY	DELEGATE
TONGAAT HULLETT	T GARNER
UNION SPINNING MILLS	C SNIJMAN

National RoBiT Committee

COMPANY	DELEGATE	ADDRESS	TELEPHONE
CBM	T EL OFF	PO BOX 2352 JHB 2000	(011) 614 2213
CBM	C COLEMAN	PO BOX 2352 JHB 2000	(011) 614 2213
CBM	B COETSEE	PO BOX 2352 JHB 2000	(011) 614 2213
CBM	G CULLEN	PO BOX 54356 DBN 4000	(031) 32 7652
CBM	R OLIVIER	PO BOX 1226 CT 8000	(021) 658 2291
CBM	A FEINSTEIN	PO BOX 1114 JHB 2000	(011) 491 6461
ENGEN	M PALMER	PO BOX 21 CT 8000	(021) 403 4911
ESKOM	G LINDEQUE	PO BOX 1091 JHB 2000	(011) 800 2911
HL&H	R COX	PO BOX 47 JHB 2000	(011) 883 4120
NAMPAK	P CAMPBELL	PO BOX 784324 SANDTON 2146	(011) 884 1418
PG BISON	L COHEN	PO BOX 2352 JHB 2000	(011) 618 1640
PROTEA ASS	A TAINTON	PO BOX 635 CT 8000	(021) 488 7922
SHELL OIL	T MCCULLOCH	PO BOX 2231 CT 8000	(021) 408 4911
SOUTHERN LIFE	A VD ZWAN	PO BOX 1114 JHB 2000	(011) 491 6404
T&N HOLDINGS	M PARRY	PO BOX 1527 DBN 4000	(031) 32 2679
UNION SPINNING	J OOSTHUIZEN	PO BOX 4032 KORSTEN PE 6014	(041) 43 1888

Staff: Consultative Business Movement

Head office

Address: PO Box 2352, Johannesburg, 2000
Telephone: (011) 614 2213
Fax: (011) 618 2079

Theuns Eloff	Colin Coleman
Debra Marsden	Renee Alberts
Ben Coetsee	Roddy Payne

Natal

Address: PO Box 54356, Durban, 4000
Telephone: (031) 32 7652
Fax: (031) 368 1756
Gary Cullen
Dominic Mitchell

Western Cape

Address: PO Box 1226, Cape Town, 8000
Telephone: (021) 658 2291
Fax: (021) 658 2182
Retief Olivier
Zorah Ebrahim

PWV

Address: PO Box 1114, Johannesburg, 2000
Telephone: (011) 491 6461
Fax: (011) 491 6452
Andrew Feinstein
Mongezi Stofile

Delegates who attended the Robit working sessions

COMPANY	DELEGATE
ABBEY HOLDINGS	J BOWMAN
ABBEY HOLDINGS	J SCHAFFER
AECI CHLOR-ALKALI	R HOLLWAY
AFROX	P JOUBERT
AIKEN & PEAT	SG MORRIS
ALEXANDER HAMILTON	A HAMILTON
ALGORAX	PO PEHLEGARD
ALUSAF	R BARBOUR
ANGLO AMERICAN	J BUYS
ANGLOVAAL	A BEADLE
ARGUS HOLDINGS	M HOFMEYR
ARUP INCORPORATED	C MCMILLAN
BTR DUNLOP SA	C COOPER
BARLOW RAND	K IRONSIDE

COMPANY	DELEGATE
BEACON SWEETS	B WALLET
BEIER INDUSTRIES	H BEIER
BELL-ESSEX ENG	C STEENEKAMP
BLUE RIBBON BAKERIES	F RICCARDI
BP SA	G BARR
BP SA	P WILKINSON
CG SMITH SUGAR	G TAYLOR
CI CARAVANS	R CARDO
CADBURY	PE BEYERS
CADBURY	M ACKHURST
CALTEX	T O'DONOVAN
CALTEX	I BONORCHIS
CALTEX	J MCKENZIE
CLARK COTTON	E BROCK
CLUTCH & BRAKE SUPP	P MYBURGH
CON ROUX CONSTR	J ROUX
CT CHAMBER OF COMM	C MCCARTHY
CT CHAMBER OF COMM	J MALONE
CT CHAMBER OF COMM	L HARTMAN
DBSA	CC MCKENZIE
DBSA	D GANZ
DBSA	M MALATSI
DBSA	J POTLOANE
DBSA	E ORBACH
DBSA	B SETAI
DBSA	J VAN ROOYEN
DELTA MOTOR CORP	A WELLINGTON
DENEYS REITZ	C WOOLLEY
DENEYS REITZ	M KAPELUS
DURBAN CORP (ELEC)	H WHITEHEAD
ENGEN	M PALMER
ENGEN	J ROBERTS

COMPANY	DELEGATE
ENVIROTECH	P KRUMM
EP BUILDING SOCIETY	K SIEBRITZ
EP BUILDING SOCIETY	R KNOTT-CRAIG
EPIC OIL MILLS	T LAVERY
ERNST & YOUNG	T WIXLEY
ESKOM	C HAZARD
ESKOM	G VENTER
ESKOM	J BRADBURY
ESKOM	M O'LEARY
EVERITE	G THOMAS
EXECUTIVE PROJECTS	B RAYNER
FABCOS	J MABUZA
FABCOS	T TEMBI
FABCOS	T KEMPSHALL
FEDLIFE	P KRIGE
FEDSURE HOLDINGS	D AVNIT
FERGUSON BROS	P FERGUSON
FIRST NATIONAL BANK	B SWART
FIRST NATIONAL BANK	P SCAIFE
GENCOR	J ENGELBRECHT
GENREC MEI	P BELL
GENREF	E MARTIN
GLASS SA	R FEHRSEN
GOLDEN ARROW BUS	B KRAUSE
GRINDROD UNIC LINES	M GRINDROD
HL&H	N MORRIS
HL&H	R COX
HAGGIE RAND	C MURRAY
HSRC	T VAN DER WALT
HULETT ALUMINIUM	D WINSHIP
HULTRANS	M NORRIS
INDUSTRIAL DEV CORP	C VAN DER MERWE

COMPANY	DELEGATE
ISLAMIC BANK	E KHARSANY
ISM	D MEISSNER
JCI	B DAVISON
JCI	B SUTHERLAND
JCI	J NEL
JCI	K MAXWELL
JCI	M HAWARDEN
JOFFE TECHNOLOGY	J JOFFE
JOHNSON WAX	B ZIEGENHAGEN
KROMCO	J KRUGER
LAMINATE INDUSTRIES	S WOOD
LAW REVIEW PROJECT	L TAGER
LIBERTY LIFE	D WHARTON-HOOD
M&R PROPERTIES	CJ LAWRENCE
M-NET	I MITI
MACSTEEL	MH HOFFMAN
MALBAK	D MCGLASHAN
MESSINA MINES	D KIRSTEN
METROPOLITAN LIFE	W PRETORIUS
MICHELIN SA	D MILLS
MURRAY & ROBERTS	A STEWART
MURRAY & ROBERTS	J RACTLIFFE
MCCARTHY GROUP	B MCCARTHY
MCCARTHY GROUP	R PARKHURST
NAMPAK	P CAMPBELL
NASIONALE PERS	H DEVENTER
NATAL BUILDING SOC	J GAFNEY
NATAL BUILDING SOC	M CHAPMAN
NATAL CHAMBER IND	J BRYCE
NATAL PORTLAND	R WEBER
NBS HOLDINGS	G CHAPMAN
NEDBANK REGIONAL	H LEENSTRA

COMPANY	DELEGATE
NEDCOR	B WEGERLE
NEDCOR	L PORTER
NEDCOR	PWC HIBBIT
NINIAN & LESTER	D MCGREGOR
NORWICH LIFE	C DAVIES
NORWICH LIFE	L FOURIE
NORWICH LIFE	S ADAMS
OVCON	JWS KAMINSKI
PAYEN COMPONENTS	D GALLOWAY
PAYEN COMPONENTS	S BRYER
PE CH OF COMMERCE	A VLOK
PE CH OF COMMERCE	F VD BERG
PG BISON	L COHEN
PG BISON	R COHEN
PLACOR	B LUBNER
PREFCOR	T ROSENBERG
PREMIER FOOD IND	C CLOETE
PREMIER FOOD IND	N FOWLER
PREMIER GROUP	P WRIGHTON
PREMIER PET FOODS	K LORING
PROTEA ASSURANCE	A TAINTON
PROTEA ASSURANCE	D MARKS
PROTEA ASSURANCE	N CRITICOS
RAIN INV CORP	G ASHMEAD
RAINBOW CHICKENS	R SOUTHEY
RAND MINE PROPERTIES	C STEYN
RDT	H MIDDLEMAN
RECKITT & COLMAN	F JACOBS
REMBRANDT GROUP	H KNOETZE
ROMATEX	J VAN COLLER
ROMATEX	L CRUTCHLEY
RUSSEL MARRIOT BOYD	AJ ARDINGTON

COMPANY	DELEGATE
SA NYLON SPINNERS	S SIMPSON
SA POST OFFICE	D MASSON
SA SUGAR ASS	M MATHEWS
SACOB	C NEWTON
SACOB	R HAYWOOD
SAFMARINE	P JAMES
SALDANHA BAY CANNING	A SILVERMAN
SANLAM	AF MARAIS
SANLAM	R HEINE
SATOUR	D HOLTZHAUSEN
SATOUR	M RAUBENHEIMER
SBDC	W THOMAS
SEIFSA	N COHEN
SHELL & BP	H JOUBERT
SHELL	T MCCULLOCH
SHELL SA	I WILLIAMS
SHELL SA	J KILROE
SHELL SA	K ROUX
SIEMENS	J TROTSKIE
SIEMENS	M SHULTZ
SIEMENS	R SANNE
SIMPSON MCKIE	D STRONG
SMITH & NEPHEW	H NEETHLING
SONDOR	L JORDAAN
SONDOR	SL GOLDMAN
SOUTHERN LIFE	A ARNOTT
SOUTHERN LIFE	EW PRYOW
SPOORNET	A FREEMANTLE
STANDARD BANK	G SMITH
STAUCH VORSTER	G TAYLOR
STAUCH VORSTER	R PHILIP
STOCKS & STOCKS	RA EDWARDS

COMPANY	DELEGATE
SYFRETS	D RENNIE
SYFRETS	E LODGE
T&N HOLDINGS	M PARRY
T&N HOLDINGS	MC PRETORIUS
TEK CORPORATION	N ORGAN
TELJOY	J POTGIETER
TIGER OATS	J FRANKEL
TIGER OATS	J MCGAHEY
TIGER WHEELS	E KEIZAN
TIMELIFE INSURANCE	B HASLAM
TIMELIFE INSURANCE	T DE MUNNIK
TIOXIDE SA	R LOUW
TONCORO	E RUTHERFORD
TONGAAT HULETT	E GARNER
TONGAAT HULETT	G HIBBERT
TOYOTA SA	T VAN DEN BERGH
TRANSNET	J UYS
TRENCOR SERVICES	C JOWELL
UAL MERCHANT BANK	G RYAN
UMGENI WATER	G ATKINSON
UNICORN LINES	M MEEHAN
UNIFRUCO	F MEINTJIES
UNILEVER SA	N CLAYTON
UNION SPINNING MILLS	CJ SNIJMAN
UNITRADE	MR HORWOOD
URBAN FOUNDATION	S VAN COLLER
WALTER HIRSCH & CO	H HIRSCH
WARNER LAMBERT	T LARGIER
WEBBER WENTZEL	B KING
WEPCOC	E EGOBODO
WEPCOC	T PASIWE
WITS BUSINESS SCHOOL	N BINEDELL

Appendix Two

Speakers at the RoBiT sessions

PWV 1 – 15 June 1992	
Roelf Meyer	Minister of Constitutional Development
Pravin Gordhan	Chair, Codesa Management Committee
Bobby Godsell	Executive Director, Industrial Relations and Public Affairs, Anglo American
Colin Coleman	National Programmes Director, CBM
PWV 2 – 8 July 1992	
Mike Rosholt	Chair, The Urban Foundation
Pravin Gordhan	Chair, Codesa Management Committee
Attie du Plessis	President, AHI
Colin Coleman	National Programmes Director, CBM
Durban – 10 July 1992	
Jacob Zuma	Deputy Secretary General, ANC
Zach de Beer	Leader, DP
Jabu Mabuza	Executive President, Fabcos
Colin Coleman	National Programmes Director, CBM
Port Elizabeth – 16 July 1992	
Sam Shilowa	Assistant General Secretary, Cosatu
Jabu Mabuza	Executive President, Fabcos
Leon Wessels	Minister of Local Government and Housing
Theuns Eloff	Executive Director, CBM
Cape Town – 24 July 1992	
Zach de Beer	Leader, DP
Marcel Golding	Deputy General Secretary, NUM
Theuns Eloff	Executive Director, CBM

Note: Portfolios listed for speakers are as at the date of the relevant session.